Discussion Manual for Student Relationships

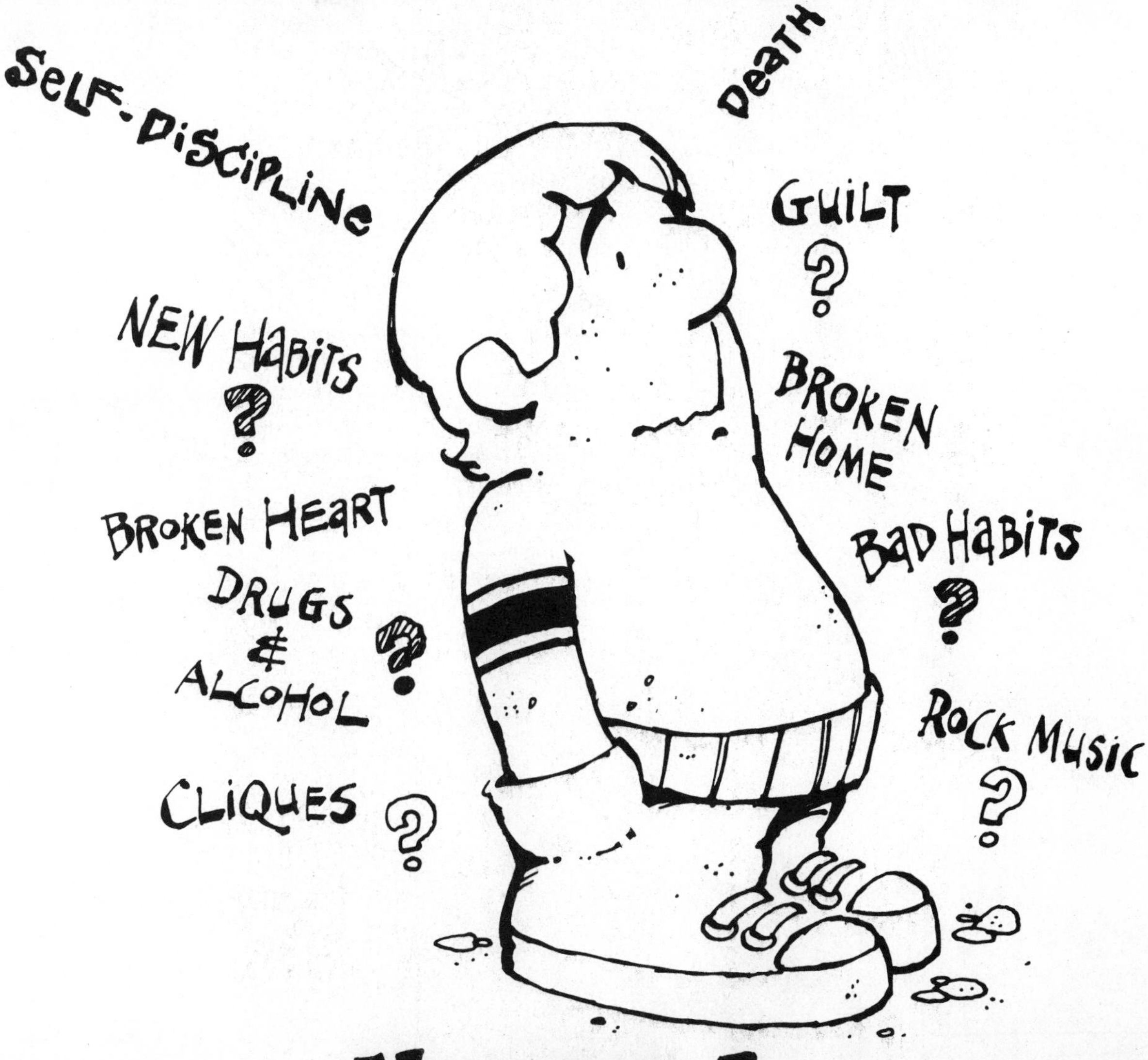

Volume 3

ISBN 0-8024-2240-3

Printed in the United States of America

Dawson McAllister

Because of the tremendous reception given the Discussion Manual for Student Relationships, Dawson introduces Volume 2, dealing with further areas of conflict for the Christian.

Dawson is a nationally renowned speaker and author. He personally pioneered Shepherd Productions, an acclaimed producer of Christian television programming and other audiovisual materials.

He is a graduate of Bethel College in Minnesota, and attended Talbot Theological Seminary in LaMirada, California.

Jim Lamb

Jim developed our art character to have a special slightly humorous and very human nature that would appeal to both sexes; and his foibles, development and growth had to be an easily identifiable pattern of behavior. Jim handles this character so that the biblical concepts, not the cartoon, predominate.

Jim has done numerous projects for several Christian publishing companies, and is polished and versatile with all artists' media. Jim is an artist/ illustrator living in Burbank, CA.

SPECIAL THANKS TO THOSE WHO HELPED DAWSON CREATE THIS MANUAL...

Helps in writing...

ED HAGUE *Youth Pastor and speaker from Athens, Georgia*

MIKE HUBER *Youth Pastor from Evergreen, Colorado*

KEN PHILLIPS *Youth Worker and speaker from Sacramento, California*

JOHN MILLER *Youth Pastor from Tucson, Arizona*

Helps in research...

ALAN HLAVKA *Youth Pastor from Wayne, Pennsylvania*

JOEL MORGAN *Production Assistant and Art Coordinator*

Calligraphy by **RAHIME A. MORGAN**

Art layout by **"ONE WAY IMAGES"** *Denver, Colorado*

Special thanks to the **STUDENTS AT RAVENS CREST CHALET "TORCHBEARERS"** *in Estes Park, Colorado for consulting and editing helps.*

DISCUSSION MANUAL for STUDENT RELATIONSHIPS

Vol. 3

The youth of America are facing problems that are seemingly insurmountable. The breakdown of the home is almost the norm for today's society. Lawlessness on the part of the young is already statistically staggering and is on the increase.

Such problems as loneliness, doubt, misuse of sex, powerful temptation, guilt, low self-esteem and other personal and relationship-oriented problems are plaguing countless thousands of people. Satan and the powers of darkness would like the student of today to think that there are no answers to the problems--except answers than man himself can invent. There could be no bigger lie.

God has clearly set down solutions to man's basic needs. He has sent Christ to pay for man's sins and to be a light to man, who is so in need of moral guidance. God has also revealed in His Word (the Bible) the basic guidelines to follow as men face the problems that life and sin bring.

God is not vague on answers to living; He speaks clearly and openly on life's issues. It is with this thought in mind that the authors conceived this manual. The authors realize that one cannot "can" answers to meet the total complexities of each person's detailed problems. However, God gives clear principles in the Bible that will work for the Christian if he will but dig them out, obey and practice them.

HOW TO USE THIS MANUAL

This Discussion Manual for Student Relationships Volume 3 can be used quite effectively as a small group Bible study tool.

The manual can also be used as a one-on-one sharing/discipleship tool. (Needless to say, some chapters are lengthier than others, so care should be taken to select specific parts of certain chapters for concentrated sharing of the biblical principles here.)

This manual can be used for your own personal Bible study--or for the personal Bible study of someone you are discipling. The manual shouldn't be given out indiscriminately, but selectively with care and concern on the part of the giver.

* QUESTIONS IN THIS MATERIAL.

There were two essential purposes in the authors' minds in the selection, style, and placement of the questions found in this manual.

FIRST, the questions are asked to provoke users to meaningful thought and discussion. Such encounters can sometimes be more helpful to the new Christian than all the rest of his/her reading of the manual.

SECOND, the questions are obviously used in some places to bring out a point or just to make Scripture a bit clearer in a specific application to the reader. Some of the questions may seem simplistic, and the answers are provided in parentheses under selective questions. But, the exercise of considering the thought in the questions is important.

* THE ART.

This manual's cartoon/illustrations were selected for visual focus on a biblical principle and not essentially for humor (although humor can be discovered in many of the illustrations). Make sure that the new believer takes a concentrated look at the artwork and thoroughly understands what is being visualized.

* MATERIAL PLACEMENT.

Each discussion chapter builds somewhat on the preceding material. It would be wise to follow this intended progression as the manual gets "deeper," unless a specific need can be met by directing the young believer to a specific discussion chapter.

Table of Contents

How to Deal with Cliques . . . . Page 1

What to Do when Your Boyfriend or Girlfriend Drops You . . . . Page 23

God's View of the Misuse of Drugs and Alcohol . . . . . . Page 53

How to Break Bad Habits . . . . Page 75

How to Develop New Healthy Habits . . . . Page 105

How to Live in a Broken Home . . . . Page 121

How to Deal with Guilt . . . . Page 143

The Christian Student and Rock Music . . . . Page 167

Disciplining Your Time . . . . Page 189

How to Face Death . . . . Page 213

How to deal with
CLIQUES

No doubt most Christian high school students have either faced or been involved in cliques. Many Christian youth groups seem to be troubled with this problem. Although Christian students claim that Christ has given them a new kind of love and caring, some willfully exclude certain people from their circle of love.

SINCE THIS IS TRUE — LET'S STUDY....

* *What is a clique?*
* *What causes cliques?*
* *Why is God not for cliques?*
* *How to be a clique breaker.*

I. WHAT IS A CLIQUE?

A clique is a small, exclusive circle of people who have common interests. Once formed, there is an unwillingness by members of the group to admit others into their circle of friendship.

* *Do you have cliques in your Christian group?*____________________
* *If so, how do you know that there is a clique?*____________________

  ____

* *Do you think you are personally involved in a clique?*________________

SUPER SPIRITUALS

The super spirituals think they are really spiritual because they know a lot about the Bible. They want to associate only with those who talk about spiritual things. They tend to look down their noses at anyone whom they judge not to be as spiritual as themselves.

Rowdies

You can detect a rowdy usually by his or her voice level. They love to group together and make fun of church singing, speakers, etc. They usually go to church only because it's the thing to do, and they are held together by their basic mockery of what goes on in the youth group.

Popular at School (Cool Ones)

This small but exclusive group is "big time" on their campus. They come to church all right, but believe that most of the kids in the youth group are social losers. Because this is their opinion, this group ignores other Christian kids at school, and they stick to themselves at church.

Me-and-My-Girlfriend-and-My-Friend-and-His-Girlfriend

This clique is hard to miss. Everyone likes to stare at them. With arms entangled, they appear to be tied to each other, holding hands in fours. Their discussion centers on, "What will be the big date on Saturday night?" Have you noticed that since love is blind, their eyes are hardly on anyone else but each other?

The Athletes

This small but powerful group of people hangs together due to their athletic greatness. Their glory is in the small subculture of sports. Since the others cannot understand sports like they can, they get together and talk about their one true love.

Just Average

They have no claim to fame per se. They are held togetherr by their need for survival. They are the only ones left. This group is usually either bitter or awestruck about the rest of the cliques. They are usually the ones most willing for the rest of the group to come closer together in "Christian love."

We Sing in the Choir Together

These are your "obviously talented" people who serve the Lord best by singing. Their whole life is built around the choir, concerts, practices, socials, etc. They are so busy singing that they don't have time for anyone else in the youth group.

SPECIAL NOTE

Of course, every Christian youth group does not have all of these groups in it. But if they do have some of them, or a variation, then God is not pleased and wants us to do something about the problem.

WHAT A CLIQUE IS NOT!

Just because you have a group of close friends does not necessarily mean you belong to a clique. God wants us to develop close friendships. You and your friends, however, should ask the following questions.

- *Do you ever catch yourself feeling that you and your friends are more "with it" than others in your youth group?*
- *Do you make it a point to get to know new students at your club or meeting?*
- *Do you ever find yourself putting down other Christians who belong to a different church or group than you?*
- *If you are talking to someone who is not one of your close friends, and one of your close friends walks in, do you immediately leave that person to go and talk with your close friends?*
- *Do you ever try to discourage someone from being involved with you and your friends because they don't fit the mold of what is acceptable to your group?*

If you had to answer "YES" to any of the above questions, or if you know someone who would have answered "YES" to any of the above questions, then you should read on in this study.

II. WHAT CAUSES CLIQUES?

Although most of us have encountered cliques, few of us have ever stopped to consider what causes them. We may react to them. We may not like them. We may be involved in one of them. But just why do they come about? The Bible seems to indicate that this misuse of friendships can be be traced to three wrong attitudes:

- *Prideful Status Seeking*
- *Fear & Insecurity*
- *Selfishness & Laziness.*

A. PRIDEFUL STATUS SEEKING

Our sin nature, which is full of pride, tells us that we must be the center of attention in social relationships. So we deceive ourselves into thinking that climbing into a higher status group will make us happier. This un-Christlike way of thinking prompts us to use people as a means of achieving higher status. After getting into this higher group, our sin nature tells us that we are really "with it," and we tend to look down on anyone who is not in the clique with us.

JESUS WAS NOT A STATUS SEEKER

When Jesus walked on this earth, He was not concerned about who accepted Him, but rather with what God wanted Him to do. Religious leaders of His day criticized Him for spending time with people of low acclaim.

Matthew 9:10-13
10) "And it happened that as He was reclining at table in the house, behold many tax-gatherers and sinners came and joined Jesus and His disciples at the table.
11) "And when the Pharisees saw this, they said to His disciples, 'Why does your Teacher eat with the tax-gatherers and sinners?'"
12) "But when He heard this, He said, 'It is not those who are healthy who need a physician, but those who are ill.
13) "'But go and learn what this means, "I desire compassion, and not sacrifice," for I did not come to call the righteous, but sinners.'"

✶ *Why is it that Jesus was not a status seeker?* ____________________

✶ *Why do you think Jesus would spend time with the down-and-outs?* __
____

✶ *What is Jesus' advice to those who look down their noses at someone seemingly "less important" than themselves?* ____________________
____

Jesus' whole life on earth was evidence that prideful status seeking goes against God's plan for our relationships with each other. That is why Paul says:

Romans 12:16
"Be of the same mind toward one another; do not be haughty in mind, but associate with the lowly. Do not be wise in your own estimation."

B. FEAR AND INSECURITY

Another reason cliques are so common among Christians today is fear and insecurity. All of us have a basic desire to feel needed and wanted. The problem is that we look too much to our friends to supply that need. The last thing we want is to lose importance and favor with our closest associates. So we often tend to "shut out" newcomers to the group because they threaten our standing and relationship in the group. We are insecure, and we fail to see ourselves as someone of importance whom God has made. Instead of trusting God, we put our security in numbers. We say to ourselves, "If they laugh at me they will have to laugh at the whole group."

Security in anything else but God is insecurity.

God explains throughout the Scriptures that real security in life is found only in Him. Speaking to the children of Israel He said:

Isaiah 31:1,3
1) "Woe to those who go down to Egypt for help, and rely on horses, and trust in chariots because they are many, and in horsemen because they are very strong, but they do not look to the Holy
3) One of Israel, nor seek the Lord! Now the Egyptians are men, and not God, and their horses are flesh and not spirit; so the Lord will stretch out His hand, and he who helps will stumble and he who is helped will fall, and all of them will come to an end together."

* *According to the above verses, what mistake did the children of Israel make when they were in need?* ______________________

____

* *Why is it a mistake to depend solely upon our friends for our security?* ______________________

____

However God does use our friends to help meet our needs. But if we have a close friendship with God and our security comes from Him, we won't have to be worried about losing or gaining friends. Our fear will be taken care of because of God's love for us.

As He says in 1 John 4:18, "There is no fear in love; but perfect love casts out fear, because fear involves punishment, and the one who fears is not perfected in love."

C. SELFISHNESS AND LAZINESS

Cliques can also be caused by selfishness and laziness. Once we reach the place that we have a close-knit group of friends around us, it is easy to become indifferent to others. Our sin nature tells that we no longer need to reach out to someone who needs us and our friends. This attitude is very selfish.

God is against this kind of thinking. Jesus wants us to know that we should not feel that we have done some great loving deed just because we have a group of friends.

He says in Matthew 5:46-47 (Living Bible) -- "If you love only those who love you, what good is that? Even scoundrels do that much. If you are friendly only to your friends, how are you different from anyone else? Even the heathen do that."

✳ Why is it no big act of love to be friends with people who care about us? ______________________________

✳ What, then, do you think Jesus was trying to get us to do? ______

____

PERSONAL APPLICATION

Write a paragraph below describing one of the three areas you have the most difficulty in; (prideful status seeking, fear and insecurity, or selfishness and laziness). Describe the circumstances, the times, the people involved, and your responses to them.

III. WHY IS GOD NOT FOR CLIQUES?

We have seen in the previous section that God's ideal for us is directly opposed to the formation of cliques. The first reason for this is that:

A. THEY GO AGAINST THE VERY FAIRNESS OF GOD

We are commanded throughout the Scriptures to imitate who God is and the principles for which He stands. For example, God says in Ephesians 5:1-2: "Therefore be imitators of God, as beloved children; and walk in love, just as Christ also loved you, and gave Himself up for us, an offering and a sacrifice to God as a fragrant aroma."

HOW DOES A CHILD IMITATE HIS FATHER?

Obviously a child cannot perfectly imitate his father in all things. He's too young, and too immature, but he can mimic his father enough so than an observer could tell that he is his father's son. We too, as Christians, are not big enough nor mature enough to perfectly imitate God. Yet we can reflect enough of His image and character that others will recognize us as being His children.

* *According to the above passage (Eph. 5:1-2), who is the example whom we can follow, if we desire to imitate God?* ______________

____

GOD IS IMPARTIAL

God's very nature goes against the attitudes and elements that form a clique. For example, God is completely impartial in his dealings with man. No person gets special treatment from God due to their looks, wealth, fame, or heritage. God described this trait of His in the passage:

Deuteronomy 10:16-19 (Living Bible)
16) "Therefore, cleanse your sinful hearts and stop your stubbornness.
17) "Jehovah your God is God of gods and Lord of lords. He is the great and mighty God, the God of terror who shows no partiality and takes no bribes.
18) He gives justice to the fatherless and widows. He loves foreigners and gives them food and clothing.
19) (You too must love foreigners, for you yourselves were foreigners in the land of Egypt.)"

* *What do the groups of people in the above verses have in common?* ______________________________

* *According to the above verses, what are the commands that God gives to his children?* ______________________________

____

GOD'S LOVE—

God is not only impartial, but He is actively loving all men. In the Bible, God shows more love than we can comprehend. It says:

Philippians 2:5-8 (Living Bible)
5) "Your attitude should be the kind that was shown us by Jesus Christ,
6) "who, though He was God, did not demand and cling to His rights as God,
7) "but laid aside His mighty power and glory, taking the disguise of a slave and becoming like men.
8)And He humbled Himself even further, going so far as actually to die a criminal's death on a cross."

* *Observe the above passage. What attitudes do you see Christ having that indicate He would never have formed a clique?*

____

____

____

____

GOD'S RIGHTS

God could have isolated and disassociated Himself from sinful man. But He didn't! Instead of clinging to His rightful "status" as God, He invaded the universe and became man. Jesus is the greatest clique breaker that has ever lived. Though unwanted by many, He broke through to man for man's own good. Then He died on a cruel cross to make a way for <u>*all*</u> *men to come to God.*

Since God's very nature is against the kind of attitudes that lead to social exclusiveness, we as His children should also avoid those same hurtful attitudes. Our common purpose as Christians should be just what God instructed in 1 John 3:16, "We know love by this, that He laid down His life for us; and we ought to lay down our lives for the brethren."

B. CLIQUES CAUSE US TO SHOW FAVORITISM TO OTHERS ON FAULTY-SHALLOW STANDARDS

As has already been mentioned, God does not show favoritism. He is absolutely fair. Cliques, on the other hand, not only show personal favoritism toward others but base that judgment on a standard that is faulty. In James we have clear explanation why God is against cliques.

James 2:1-10

1) *"My brethren, do not hold your faith in our glorious Lord Jesus Christ with an attitude of personal favoritism.*

2) *"For if a man comes into your assembly with a gold ring and dressed in fine clothes, and there also comes in a poor man in dirty clothes,*
3) *"and you pay special attention to the one who is wearing the fine clothes, and say, 'You sit here in a good place,' and you say to the poor man, 'You stand over there, or sit down by my footstool,'*
4) *"have you not made distinctions among yourselves, and become judges with evil motives?*

5) *"Listen, my beloved brethren: did not God choose the poor of this world to be rich in faith and heirs of the kingdom which He promised to those who love Him?*
6) *"But you have dishonored the poor man. Is it not the rich who oppress you and personally drag you into court?*
7) *"Do they not blaspheme the fair name by which you have been called?*

8) *"If, however, you are fulfilling the royal law, according to the Scripture, 'You shall love your neighbor as yourself,' you are doing well.*
9) *"But if you show partiality, you are committing sin and are convicted by the law as transgressors.*

10) *"For whoever keeps the who law and yet stumbles in one point, he has become guilty of all."*

* *What problem did the Christians in James' day have?* ____________

____

* *What was their faulty standard for showing this favoritism?* ______

____

* *God says that riches are a faulty standard on which to judge a person. What are some other shallow reasons why people pick others to be in their clique?* ____________________

____

____

* *According to verses 8-10, how serious does God view an attitude of personal favoritism?* ____________________

____

____

____

A MODERN PARAPHRASE AND PERSONAL APPLICATION

In order to make James 2:1-10 come alive for our situation today, rewrite it using your youth group as the basis and using your own words to express James' thoughts and principles.

C. CLIQUES CAN BE CRUEL TO THE PEOPLE REJECTED BY THE GROUP

Since cliques by their very definition are exclusive and judgmental, they quickly become cruel to the people outside the group. This cruelty is shown in several different ways. Cliques can hurt the very people who need our love and help the most. Usually people within a clique feel that they are the most "with it" people around. When they look at others, they see them as inferior, or not really worth their attention. Though it may be true that those outsiders are not as "sharp" as we would like, God still desires that we love them and allow them to share in our lives.

In Christ's time there was no greater friction between any two cliques than that between the Jews and the Samaritans. The Samaritans were half-Jews who believed that they too had an adequate place of worship (John 4:20). The Jews felt that they were by far superior to the Samaritans. Jesus told a real-life story to demonstrate that the "neighbor" whom He wants us to love and help is anyone with whom we come in contact and who has a need.

Luke 10:30-37

30) "Jesus replied and said, 'A certain man was going down from Jerusalem to Jericho; and he fell among robbers, and they stripped him and beat him, and went off leaving him half dead.

31) "And by chance a certain priest was going down on that road, and when he saw him, he passed by on the other side.

32) "And likewise a Levite also, when he came to the place and saw him, passed by on the other side.

33) "But a certain Samaritan, who was on a journey, came upon him; and when he saw him, he felt compassion,

34) "and came to him, and bandaged up his wounds, pouring oil and wine on them; and he put him on his own beast, and brought him to an inn, and took care of him.

35) "And on the next day, he took out two denarii and gave them to the innkeeper and said, 'Take care of him; and whatever more you spend, when I return, I will repay you.'

36) "Which of these three do you think proved to be a neighbor to the man who fell into the robbers' hands?

37) "And he said, 'The one who showed mercy toward him." And Jesus said to him, 'Go and do the same.'"

* *What attitudes were expressed by the men who passed by the man in need?* ______________________________

____

* *Was there anything pleasing or attractive about the hurt man that would have caused the Samaritan to want to stop?* ________

____

* *What attitude did the Samaritan express in meeting the man's needs?* ______________________________

____

No doubt each of us knows people who are not naturally attractive to us. However, many of these people have emotional and spiritual needs and pains. God does not want us to further hurt these people through excluding them. He wants us to reach out to them and express compassion in meeting their needs.

No one can be rejected by a group for very long before he begins to realize that he is being rejected. This often results in a negative response from the person being "put off." Not only is this divisive to the Body of Christ, but it may also seriously hinder that person's growth in Christ. Paul warned the Galatian Christians:

Galatians 5:14-15
"For the whole Law is fulfilled in one word, in the statement, 'You shall love your neighbor as yourself.' But if you bite and devour one another, take care lest you be consumed by one another."

Such backbiting and "devouring" are just what Satan wants to happen. Nothing could please him more. But God wants us to build up one another and to encourage each other. As Romans 13:10 states, "Love does no wrong to a neighbor; love therefore is the fulfillment of the law."

Christians are not the only people to be suffering from the bad effects of exclusiveness. Those who have never met Christ can be and often are more vicious to one another.

Jesus taught that one of the most powerful ways a non-Christian is influenced to come to Christ is through the love that he sees between Christians. In John 13:34-35, He said, "A new commandment I give to you, that you love one another, even as I have loved you, that you also love one another. By this all men will know that you are My disciples, if you have love for one another."

* *According to the above passage, what is the one proof by which people will know that we love Jesus?* ______________________

____

____

It is sad when a
non-Christian comes
to our group seeking love
and finds that, due to our disobedience,
we act just like the very people who have hurt them.
These people look at our actions to see if there is living proof that Christ is real. If, on the one hand, we say that Christ gives us love and, on the other hand, we do not practice love, but rather are cliquish and cruel, we are living a lie.

GOD IS VERY CLEAR

God is very clear as to how important it is to actually live the truth. He tells us how important in 1 John 3:17-18 and 1 John 4:20.

1 John 3:17-18
17) "But whoever has the world's goods, and beholds his brother in need and closes his heart against him, how does the love of God abide in him?
18) "Little children, let us not love with word or with tongue, but in deed and truth."

1 John 4:20
"If some one says, 'I love God,' and hates his brother, he is a liar; for the one who does not love his brother whom he has seen, cannot love God whom he has not seen."

It is obvious from all of this, that God is against the misuse of friendships. He sees it as an affront to His very nature of fairness and love. God has never wanted Christians to show partiality based upon shallow standards. He knows that this practice is harmful to the people who most need to experience being loved. God wants you to demonstrate that the Christian life really works and that it is the only way to live.

IV. HOW TO BE A CLIQUE BREAKER

A. TO THOSE WHO THINK THEY MIGHT BE INVOLVED IN A CLIQUE

1. *First you need to realize that God is grieved by your actions. God sees us as we really are and the attitudes that go against Him. You will find yourself with a closer walk with God if you will confess your sin of pride and favoritism.*

2. *God's plan is for you to show love and concern to other people even though they may not be as "with it" as you are. Jesus already loves them, so by an act of faith you need to begin to show love too. As you begin to love others by faith, you will find that experience more fulfilling and secure than the clique that you once thought so important.*

3. *When Jesus came upon a situation that wasn't right (such as the money changers in the Temple), He did something about it. It may be up to you to say something to those people who are in your clique. Be sure to do it with God's goodness and love.*

B. TO THOSE WHO HAVE BEEN SHUT OUT BY A CLIQUE

1. *Know that true success comes from drawing close to God, not from our friends. You may feel angry, insecure, or left out, because you cannot break into a clique. However, this time of your life may actually be a time of great growth and understanding. If the experience of being left out of a group only pushes you all the more to a personal relationship with God, then the pain of this rejection will be well worth it. The key to successful living is found when we understand that popularity is not nearly so valuable as a close relationship with Jesus Christ.*

SEEING FOLKS FOR WHO THEY REALLY ARE

2. *It may be easy for you, due to the cliques around you, to become withdrawn, bitter, and hostile toward those inside the select group. Usually those who have developed these attitudes find themselves running to the youth leader or others to complain about their rejection. But this complaining and grumbling is not really God's plan for you to become a clique breaker. He wants you to be part of the solution, not part of the problem. He wants you to put on a heart of compassion for those who are in the clique. Keep in mind that they too have personal needs, some of which are expressed even through being in their clique. Seek ways to minister to their fears, pride, selfishness, loneliness, and other needs. It is important that we be praying for these people. You will find it impossible to remain bitter toward someone for whom you are praying.*

Love is Never easy

Love is never easy. It is not a gushy and warm feeling. Love will keep on expressing kindness and concern toward these people even if it takes a while for them to respond.

IN CONCLUSION....

Although cliques are ugly and hurtful, they do develop within many Christian groups. Perhaps your own youth group has this problem. You must realize that God's desire for you is that you be an example of love and trust in Him.

> *GOD HAS GIVEN US PRINCIPLES FOR THEIR PREVENTION AND CURE.*

It is important to allow God to keep us from entering a clique. You must realize that God's desire for you is to be an example of love and trust in Him.

You must realize that it is never easy to love all types of people as God commands, but with Christ living within you, He will give you the love that you will need, which will never die out.

NOTES

What to do when your

BOYFRIEND OR GIRLFRIEND "DROPS YOU"

For many people there is no greater emotional pain than the devastating feeling of being "dropped," or rejected, by a boyfriend or girlfriend. Our desire to love and be loved is intense and personal. Therefore when someone from the opposite sex rejects that love, a deep sense of disappointment and failure can overwhelm our lives.

Virtually everyone at one time or another faces the "broken heart" experience of being rejected by a boyfriend or girlfriend. All of us know that our dating relationships don't always turn out the way we want them to. Along with love and fulfillment, we sometimes experience pain.

<u>God's Word is not a fairy-tale book</u>. <u>God is concerned and has a realistic view about the hurt and confusion that come our way in life</u>. The Bible proclaims throughout its text clear advice on what to do when our heart is crushed by a shattered romance.

LET'S TAKE A LOOK AT "SOUND ADVICE" GOD WANTS US TO FOLLOW WHEN OUR HEART IS BROKEN

I. ONE BIT OF SOUND ADVICE THAT GOD GIVES US WHEN OUR HEART IS BROKEN IS TO BE THANKFUL THAT GOD IS STILL DEALING WITH US IN HIS PERFECT LOVE

How difficult it is to be thankful and full of joy when the person who meant so much to us now seems so distant and unconcerned about our deepest needs. But God very clearly states that we, in fact, should and can be thankful even in the middle of this painful ordeal.

He spoke of this attitude of thankfulness in:

1 Thessalonians 5:16-18 (Living Bible)
16) "Always be joyful.
17) "Always keep on praying.
18) "No matter what happens, always be thankful, for this is God's will for you who belong to Christ Jesus."

God says in the above passage that we should "always be joyful" and "always be thankful, no matter what happens".

* *Since "always" and "no matter what happens" include having a broken heart, do you think it is possible to be joyful and thankful even when we've been hurt by someone we love?* ______________________________

____

"JOYFUL OVER GOD'S PERFECT LOVE"

There are many reasons why we can be both joyful and thankful at what appears to be an awful experience. Perhaps the main reason stems from the fact that God is still dealing with us in His perfect love.

It's at a time like this that we can begin to think that God doesn't really love us or that He has forgotten us. We may at times think He is just too big to be concerned about the details of our lives. But the Bible tells us that this simply isn't so.

Romans 8:38-39 (Living Bible)
38) "For I am convinced that nothing can ever separate us from His love. Death can't, and life can't. The angels won't, and all the powers of hell itself cannot keep God's love away. Our fears for today, our worries about tomorrow,
39) "or where we are - high above the sky, or in the deepest ocean - nothing will ever be able to separate us from the love of God demonstrated by our Lord Jesus Christ when He died for us."

* *Let's assume that the emotional pain of being rejected was so great that you actually died of a "broken heart." According to Romans 8:38, would your death separate you from God's love?*

____

* *There is no doubt that ending a relationship can be an extremely painful time. But let's suppose (if you can!) your life is twenty times more awful than it is now. According to Romans 8:38, would this separate you from God's great love?* __________

____

Let's assume that Satan unleased all his demonic powers upon you, causing fear, persecution, and all kinds of personal agony. According to Romans 8:38, would Satan's activities separate you from God's love? ______________________________

____

According to the passage Romans 8:38-39, is there anything that has or might still happen between you and your boyfriend/girl-friend that could separate you from God's perfect love? ________

____

Answer: *No!* *God loves us no matter what may happen in our lives. Even when our hopes are shattered, God is still dealing with us in His love. He is not in the failing business!*

JOY OVER GOD'S UNWILLINGNESS TO FORGET US

It's easy for us to say in our heads, "Yes, God loves me", but at the same time still feel in our hearts that He has forgotten us or doesn't really care about our shattered lives.

The Children of Israel began to feel the same way in the midst of their problems. God tenderly straightened them out on the matter. He wants us to apply to our lives what He told them.

The example of the Children of Israel is found in:

Isaiah 49:14-16
14) "But Zion said, 'The Lord has forsaken me, and the Lord has forgotten me.'
15) "Can a woman forget her nursing child, and have no compassion on the son of her womb? Even these may forget, but I will not forget you.
16) "Behold, I have inscribed you on the palms of My hands; your walls are continually before Me."

How many mothers do you know who would walk off and desert their newborn children? (No doubt you have read about a few mothers who have done this, but not very many.) God says some mothers may forget their children, but He will never forget you.

HAVE YOU EVER FOUND YOURSELF WITHOUT A PIECE OF PAPER TO WRITE DOWN SOMETHING IMPORTANT? If it was really important you probably wrote it on the palm of your hand. God is spirit and doesn't have hands as we understand them, but in the passage in Isaiah 49:14-16, He wants us to know that His great mind is continually concentrating on us!

God even promises us a special love and closeness when our hearts are broken and we are confused as to what is taking place. He says in

Psalm 34:18
"The Lord is near to the brokenhearted, and saves those who are crushed in spirit."

HIS LOVING CLOSENESS IS PROMISED TO US AT JUST THE TIME WE SEEM TO NEED IT THE MOST.

Despite what our feelings may tell us, we can know that God's intimacy, love, and comfort are most effective when we feel crushed, no matter how great the pain.

Once we understand more of what God is like, we can say with the suffering Job:

Job 23:8-10
8)"Behold, I go forward but He is not there, and backward, but I cannot perceive Him;
9) "when He acts on the left, I cannot behold Him; He turns on the right, I cannot see Him.
10) "But He knows the way I take; when He has tried me, I shall come forth as gold."

II. GOD HAS ANOTHER PIECE OF SOUND ADVICE FOR US WHEN OUR HEARTS ARE BROKEN BY OUR BOYFRIEND OR GIRLFRIEND. HE SAYS IT WOULD BE WISE TO ACCEPT HIS TOTAL PLAN FOR US IN THIS MATTER.

God has a big advantage over us as finite people. We are able to see our past and present but have very little knowledge about specific circumstances of our future. God, on the other hand, sees the entire length of our lives. He is aware of the past, the present, and even the future.

Since this is true, nothing takes Him by surprise--not even the heartbreak of losing a boyfriend or girlfriend. God is not surprised and has a plan, which He uses throughout the entire situation. It is never God's desire to make us miserable. He always has our best interests at heart!

Because God's knowledge of our lives is far superior to our own, and because He has a purpose (rooted in His love) for all that happens to us, it would help us a great deal to look at life and its circumstances from His perspective. God says:

Proverbs 3:5-6

5) "Trust in the Lord with all your heart, and do not lean on your own understanding.

6) "In all your ways acknowledge Him, and He will make your paths straight."

* *Why do you think that God wants us to trust Him with* ***all*** *our hearts?* ______________________________

* *Why does God say that although we can use our minds, we aren't to totally lean on our own understanding?* ______________________________

____

* *What does the passage (Proverbs 3:5-6) mean when it says, "In all your ways acknowledge Him"?* ______________________________

____

According to the passage (Proverbs 3:5-6), if we trust God with all our hearts, don't lean on our own understanding, and acknowledge

* Him in all our ways, what is God's promise to us?________________

____

When the Children of Israel began to wonder if God really knew what He was doing, He made a fantastic promise to them. This promise still holds true in our lives today. He told them:

Jeremiah 29:11
"'For I know the plans that I have for you,' declares the Lord, 'plans for welfare and not for calamity to give you a future and a hope.'"

GOD HAS COMPLETE WISDOM

At times, we can begin to wonder why God has allowed us to be hurt. We were looking for love and ended up with only pain and heartache. It's at times like these that we need to remember that God has infinite wisdom and knowledge. He knows what's best for us better than we do ourselves! He said:

Isaiah 55:8-9
8) "'For my thoughts are not your thoughts, neither are your ways My ways,' declares the Lord.
9) "'For as the heavens are higher than the earth, so are My ways higher than your ways, and My thoughts than your thoughts.'"

God is in His own great realm of thinking when it comes to knowledge and wisdom. You and I, on the other hand, are not always able to comprehend His ways. But by looking at Scripture, we can still think of some reasons as to what He might be accomplishing through the loss of our boyfriend or girlfriend.

WHAT GOD MIGHT BE ACCOMPLISHING THROUGH THE LOSS OF OUR BOYFRIEND OR GIRLFRIEND:

- *He may be teaching us what it means to be hurt.*
- *He may be allowing this trial to help our faith develop real endurance.*
- *He may be teaching us how to love others unconditionally.*
- *He may be teaching us what it means to be humble.*
- *He may want us to spend more time in a particular ministry.*
- *He may want us to spend more time falling in love with Him.*
- *He may be pointing out weak areas that need to be developed before we consider marriage.*
- *He may be teaching us to trust Him with everything (even our date lives).*

III. ANOTHER PIECE OF SOUND ADVICE THAT GOD WANTS US TO FOLLOW UPON REALIZING HIS LOVE AND PLAN FOR US, IS TO ASK OURSELVES SOME HARD QUESTIONS ABOUT OUR RELATIONSHIP WITH OUR FORMER BOYFRIEND OR GIRLFRIEND.

When we go through the pain of being dropped by someone we care for, we often tend to react by going to one of two extremes. Either we place the blame for what has happened totally on ourselves or totally on the other person. God wants us to have a realistic view of what happened. He wants us to have His balanced perspective of each other's actions and weaknesses in the relationship.

He explains to us:

Proverbs 21:2
"Every man's way is right in his own eyes, but the Lord weighs the hearts."

* *According to the above verse, why is it important to let God weigh our hearts after a close relationship has come to an end?* ________

____

There is little doubt that we (as sinful humans) practice some real injustices and inconsiderations toward the people we date. These injustices could have caused the other person to break off the dating relationship with us.

Be Realistic

God wants us to be realistic with ourselves about our past failures and sins. Losing our boyfriend or girlfriend could be a blessing in disguise if it forces us to deal with sin areas that have not been dealt with.

A Failure Inventory Test

Here is just a small list of attitudes or activities that may cause our boyfriend or girlfriend to break up with us.

- *Failure to communicate openly*
- *Insensitivity towards the other's feelings*
- *Too possessive*
- *Selfishness*
- *Too physical - sexually*
- *Little spiritual leadership or response*
- *Disrespect*
- *Obnoxiousness*
- *Lack of personal hygiene*
- *Little mannerisms*
- *Dishonesty*

GOD DOES NOT WANT US TO BE MORBIDLY INTROSPECTIVE AND DOWN ON OURSELVES FOR PAST FAILURE AND SIN.

But at the same time, He does want us to confess our wrong, deal with it, and continue to grow to be more like Christ. It might be wise for us to stop at this point and ask God to reveal to us those glaring weaknesses that may have been instrumental in causing our boyfriend or girlfriend to break up with us.

We ought to be able to say with David:

Psalm 139:23-24
23) "Search me, O God, and know my heart; try me and know my anxious thoughts;
24) "and see if there be any hurtful way in me, and lead me in the everlasting way."

If we have dealt with these past failures by confessing our sin before God and have sought forgiveness from the person for any wrong we have done toward him, we then should accept ourselves for who we are and not let past failures cripple us for the future.

IF WE HAVE DEALT WITH THE PAST WE CAN LIVE IN THE PRESENT

The apostle Paul, moved by the Holy Spirit, understood how important it is to live in the present and not be paralyzed by what took place in the past. He said:

Philippians 3:13-14
13) "Brethren, I do not regard myself as having laid hold of it yet; but one thing I do: forgetting what lies behind and reaching forward to what lies ahead,
14) "I press on toward the goal for the prize of the upward call of God in Christ Jesus."

Paul realized he was far from perfect. He had a long way to go before he became like Jesus Christ.

* *According to the above passage, even though he had failed in the past, how did he now view his failures?* ______________________

____

* *What was the one thing the apostle Paul said he did in regard to his past mistakes?* ______________________

____

* *What was the goal that Paul was so earnestly seeking, according to verse 14?* ______________________

It is always difficult to squarely face our own sins and past failures. But it is necessary to do so if we are to grow as a result of these mistakes. It takes great courage and character to admit our weaknesses, but if we do, we can be sure we are on the road to maturity in Christ.

Proverbs 15:32-33 says, "He who neglects discipline despises himself, but he who listens to reproof acquires understanding. The fear of the Lord is the instruction for wisdom, and before honor comes humility."

IV. GOD HAS FURTHER ADVICE FOR US WHEN WE ARE DROPPED BY OUR BOYFRIEND OR GIRLFRIEND. HE WANTS US, BY HIS POWER, TO BE GRACIOUS AND LOVING TO THE ONE WHO HAS HURT US.

The first reaction that most of us have when hurt by someone else is to attempt defending ourselves to others.

It is easy to go to our friends and tell them our slanted story as to why the relationship ended. God does want us to seek counsel from our Christian friends. However, He doesn't want us to bad-mouth our former boyfriend or girlfriend to others. The Bible tells us:

Proverbs 17:9
"He who covers a transgression seeks love, but he who repeats a matter separates intimate friends" (emphasis added).

* *How can talking behind someone's back "separate intimate friends"?*

____

____

____

HURTING OTHERS

Our sinful natures seem constantly to want involvement in things that harm other people and ourselves.

For this reason we must constantly rely on the Holy Spirit's power to guard us from bitterness and anger. Instead of allowing our selfish natures to rule our lives during this difficult time, God wants us, through His power, to treat our former boyfriend or girlfriend with kindness and graciousness.
God explains the type of attitude we should have:

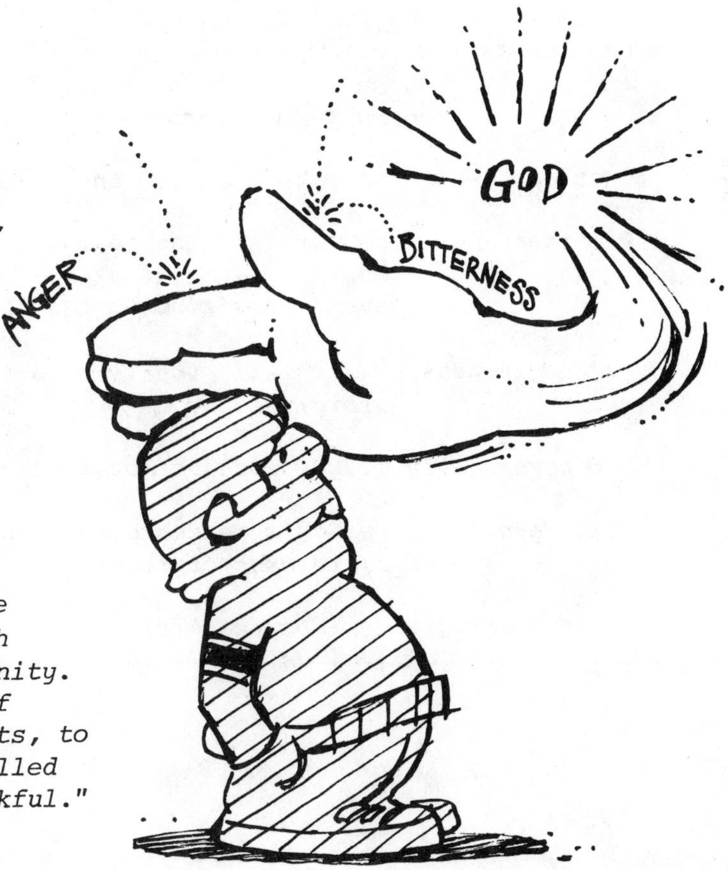

Colossians 3:12-15
12) "And so, as those who have been chosen of God, holy and beloved, put on a heart of compassion, kindness, humility, gentleness and patience;
13) "bearing with one another, and forgiving each other, whoever has a complaint against anyone; just as the Lord forgave you, so also should you.
14) "And beyond all these things put on love, which is the perfect bond of unity.
15) "And let the peace of Christ rule in your hearts, to which indeed you were called in one body; and be thankful."

This passage in Colossians 3 gives us a clear description of the type of attitude God want us to develop towards our former boyfriend or girlfriend. In the midst of our heartbreak, God can enable us to demonstrate tremendous maturity and concern toward the person we once dated.

ATTITUDE INVENTORY CHECK

Even though you have been deeply hurt, are you still willing to show your former boyfriend or girlfriend----

- *Compassion - a deep tenderness and concern for his well being and happiness.*
- *Kindness - no matter how unkind he is to you.*
- *Humility - admit your mistakes and let him know how much you appreciate his friendship.*
- *Gentleness - just because you are no longer dating him doesn't mean he no longer has needs. He doesn't need sarcasm or harsh words from you.*
- *Patience - it may take time for the pain and resentment to heal.*
- *Forbearance - you are willing to bear with him no matter how bad he treated you; resist the desire to get even, realizing he has injured feelings also.*
- *Forgiveness - after all, your sin hurt God deeply, and He has forgiven you!*
- *Love - even if you receive nothing in return.*
- *Peace - allow God's peace to rule in your heart in place of bitterness or resentment.*
- *Thanksgiving - be thankful, remember God always deals with us in His love.*

REVENGE

When our hearts have been crushed by someone who once cared for us, it is easy for the love we once had for that person to turn to hate. When this happens, our trampled pride will program our emotions with one thought...

The reasoning--"since this person has been so inconsiderate and unloving toward me, he deserves the same treatment in return. I will see that he is justly punished for the hurt he has caused me."

God, however, does not look at things this way. He gives us His perspective:

Romans 12:19-21

19) "Never take your own revenge, beloved, but leave room for the wrath of God, for it is written, 'Vengeance is Mine, I will repay,' says the Lo

20) "But if your enemy is hungry, feed him, and if he is thirsty, give him a drink; for in so doing you will heap burning coals upon his head.'

21) "Do not be overcome by evil, but overcome evil with good."

* *Why does it make more sense to let God repay those who have hurt us, rather than trying to get even ourselves?* ___________

____

____

* *According to verse 20, how does God want us to respond to our former boyfriend or girlfriend?* ___________________

____

____

* *According to verse 20, what type of an impact will your kindness have on his life?* ___________________________

____

____

* *What is God's command in verse 21?* ___________________

____

____

WATCH OUT FOR BITTERNESS

Bitterness is our biggest enemy when we have been rejected by someone who once cared for us. If we allow it to grip our lives, it will only prolong the agony and ruin what is left of the friendship we once had.

God wants us to grow from this experience and avoid the snare of bitterness. He advises us:

Hebrews 12:15 (Living Bible)
"Look after each other so that not one of you will fail to find God's best blessings. Watch out that no bitterness takes root among you, for as it springs up it causes deep trouble, hurting many in their spiritual lives."

* *How can bitterness cause deep trouble and hurt many?* ______________

____

____

____

<u>BECAUSE BITTERNESS IS SO DEVASTATING,</u>
<u>GOD WANTS US TO AVOID IT AT ANY COST</u>

God wants us to learn how to be gracious and loving no matter how others treat us. Many times, it will take an act of the will on our part to accomplish this. Whenever bad memories hit, instead of becoming angry or bitter try praying for the person.

V. GOD PERSONALLY WANTS TO FILL THE VOID IN OUR LIFE

After a boyfriend or girlfriend drops us, God wants to further help us by personally filling the void that is in our lives. <u>Upon losing our boyfriend or girlfriend, it becomes obvious to us the number of hours we spent with them and/or spent time thinking about them</u>. Now we have that extra time on our hands. That time must be filled with some things or someone.

God Himself would like to fill the emptiness with His great love and presence.

It is easy when we are in love with someone to think that he/she is really the key to our happiness. This of course is a myth. Although God can use the person we date or marry to help us be fulfilled, real meaning comes only when we have a moment by moment walk with God Himself. Jesus made this clear when He prayed to the Father:

John 17:3
"And this is eternal life, that they may know Thee, the only true God, and Jesus Christ whom Thou hast sent."

* *According to this verse, Jesus said that life eternal, or eternal life, was based on what?* ______________________________

____

When someone leaves us, especially someone we trusted so much, we are forced into rethinking where our relationship with Jesus Christ really stands.

God wants us to pursue after Him, the "eternal Lover," with even more fervor than we sought after the love and affection of our boyfriend or girlfriend.

King David was at a time of great disappointment in his life. Someone whom he loved (his son) had rebelled against and deserted him. But in the middle of the terrible heartbreak of being rejected by his son, he was able to say to God:

Psalm 63:1
"O God, Thou art my God. I shall seek Thee earnestly; my soul thirsts for Thee, my flesh yearns for Thee, in a dry and weary land where there is no water."

- *How personal did David think God was to Him?* ______________________

____

- *How intense was David's seeking and desire for God?* ______________

____

David was so much in love with God that he longed just to spend time with Him and counted the times with the Lord to be, by far, the greatest events of his life. He said to the Lord:

Psalm 84:10
"For a day in Thy courts is better than a thousand outside. I would rather stand at the threshold of the house of my God, than dwell in tents of wickedness."

God wants us to have boyfriends and girlfriends, but He wants us to get to the place that we desire to be with Him even more than we long to be with the person we love the most on this earth.

Once we've had the props knocked out from under us, we find that the Lord not only picks us up, but also becomes our intimate love forever.

FREE TO LOVE UNCONDITIONALLY

<u>WE ARE THEN FREE TO LOVE OTHERS UNCONDITIONALLY</u>,
knowing that even if everyone else leaves us
we'll have a friend who sticks closer than a brother.

God is not a fickle lover. He greatly desires to not only spend time with us but also to satisfy our every need. The Lord, however, wants us to pursue Him even as He pursues us. To the one who makes an attempt to spend time with God, the promise is given that He will respond in great measure. It's no wonder that the prophet Hosea could say:

Hosea 6:3 (Living Bible)
"Oh, that we might know the Lord! Let us press on to know him, and he will respond to us as surely as the coming of dawn or the rain of early spring."

If in this time of rejection and disappointment, we can let the Lord fill the void in our lives, we will be able to experience the greatest truth of all time. The truth is that people may come and go, but God is the constant lover who can make all our lives more than worth living.

Psalm 34:8
"O taste and see that the Lord is good; how blessed is the man who takes refuge in Him."

LET'S REVIEW FOR A MOMENT...

We can know that when heartbreak comes from being dropped by our boyfriend or girlfriend we should--

- *BE THANKFUL that God is still dealing with us in His perfect love.*
- *BE WILLING to accept His total plan for us in the matter.*
- *ASK ourselves some hard questions about our relationship with our former boyfriend or girlfriend.*
- *BE GRACIOUS and LOVING toward the one who dropped us.*
- *LET GOD FILL the VOID left by our boyfriend or girlfriend.*

We can faithfully do all the above steps and still at times find ourselves depressed and heartbroken. It is easy for us to crush our emotions, but not easy to see them once again healed. If this is true in our lives, God has some sound advice for us when we still ache emotionally from being rejected by our boyfriend or girlfriend. GOD HAS THE SOLUTION!

VI. HONESTLY AND OPENLY SHOWING GOD OUR TEARS AND BROKENESS IS WHAT HE COUNSELS US TO DO.

Some Christians feel that perhaps it is less than spiritual to pour out our tears before the Lord. They look at is as a sign of self-centeredness or weakness to let our emotions, doubts, and fears be unveiled before Christ. This less-than-honest mask of courage is not portrayed in the Bible as the way God would have us to deal with Him. Since God knows all about us and knows our every thought, He is not the least bit fooled by the suppression of our true feelings.

God is a God of sympathy. As Scripture points out in Psalm 111:4, the Lord is gracious and full of compassion. Great men and women of God throughout history have found Him to be sympathetic and helpful in their many different moods and needs.

King David, who made it his life goal to be a man after God's own heart, was also a man who wasn't afraid to let God see and hear his honest emotions. At one point in his life, he said this to the Lord:

Psalm 6:4-7 (Living Bible)
"Come, O Lord, and make me well. In your kindness save me. For if I die I cannot give you glory by praising you before my friends. I am worn out with pain; every night my pillow is wet with tears. My eyes are growing old and dim with grief because of all my enemies."

* *According to the above verses, just how desperate was David before the Lord?* ____________________
* *What part of God's character did David appeal to?* ____________________
* *What was David's main emotional need that he voiced before the Lord?* ____________________

CAST OUR SORROW ON JESUS

David had become weary with his own tears and heartache. Evidently, he didn't have the power in and of himself to solve the need. Consequently, he simply dumped all of his sorrow right on the Lord. This is exactly what the Lord wants us to do if the tears and the hurts keep occurring.

SOME HONEST STATEMENTS:

Here are some honest statements that we could share with the Lord that reveal our true emotions:

"Lord, I feel my boyfriend/girlfriend cheated me and I feel angry - Lord, soften my anger."

"Lord, since we broke up I haven't cared about anyone. I've been very rude to many people. Help me not to be so self-centered."

"Lord, since my boyfriend/girlfriend left me, I feel like a loser - help me to see that I'm not a loser in your eyes."

"Lord, since I've been dropped, I have real fears about going out with anyone else - Lord, give me courage."

"Lord, I'm so preoccupied with my depression that I can't be creative in other important areas of my life - I need Your help."

"Lord, there's so much emptiness in my life since my boyfriend/girlfriend is gone. I just sort of feel numb - please help me to snap out of it."

God deals with us when we assure Him honestly that we are desperate. It is possible to be wanting to do the Lord's will and still be in great emotional need.

If we do find ourselves in that need, He will answer our desperate request and meet the needs of our honest emotion. David shared his real pain. We can share our pain with the Lord too. We can say with David:

Psalm 56:8-9 (Living Bible)
8) "You have seen me tossing and turning through the night. You have collected all my tears and preserved them in your bottle! You have recorded every one in your book.
9) "The very day I call for help, the tide of battle turns. My enemies flee! This one thing I know: God is for me!"

We too can be assured of the victory that David received from the Lord.

VII. GOD HAS A FINAL BIT OF ADVICE FOR US TO FOLLOW WHEN WE ARE REJECTED BY SOMEONE WE LOVE. HE WANTS US TO GET UP FROM OUR PAIN, TRUSTING HIM TO REBUILD OUR LIVES WITH NEW JOYS, ADVENTURES, AND BLESSINGS.

There finally comes a time when, after being hurt by others, we must get up and trust God to get us powerfully living again. God does not want us to wallow in pain and hurt for long periods of time. It's a part of God's great plan for us to be happy.

WE MUST FINALLY COME TO THE CONCLUSION
THAT GOD IS GOING TO ENCOURAGE US IN A TANGIBLE WAY.

There is a fantastic promise given us in:

Psalm 27:13-14
13) "I would have despaired unless I had believed that I would see the goodness of the Lord in the land of the living.
14) "Wait for the Lord; be strong, and let your heart take courage; Yes, wait for the Lord."

* *What kept the psalmist going when things were going so badly for him?* ______________________________

* *According to the above verses, what two things can we do to get off of dead center with our emotions?* ______________________________

____

Some people spend a tremendous amount of time thinking of ways to get back at their previous boyfriends or girlfriends. However, if we are to freely and spontaneously give to others, we must be able to entrust God with our hearts and our former dates' feelings towards us.

There are some ideas found in Psalm 127:1-3 that could apply to our date life or previous boyfriend or girlfriend:

Verse	Dating Application
1a - Unless the Lord builds the house, they labor in vain who build it	*Unless the Lord builds the date life, he who tries to make it work, works hard for nothing.*
1b - Unless the Lord, guards the city, the watchman keeps awake in vain.	*Unless the Lord protects the dating relationship and the feelings involved, we can try all we want and will fail.*
2 - It is vain for you to rise up early, to retire late, to eat the bread of painful labors; for He gives to His beloved even in his sleep.	*It's silly to try to win back a boyfriend or girlfriend, without the Lord at work for us. It will just be a painful experience. If God wants to, He can wake up our former boyfriend or girlfriend in the middle of the night and give him/her a whole new love for us.*

Ultimately, it's the Lord who can give us the power to start living again and trusting Him for great things to happen in our lives. Psalm 3:3 explains this idea even further:

Psalm 3:3
"But Thou, O Lord, art a shield about me, my glory, and the One who lifts my head."

*What do you think "God is a shield about me" means? ______________

____

____

*What other act of love does God promise to do in our lives? ______

____

____

Only with God's help can we turn from thoughts and moods that are destructive to our growth and be led into His way of thinking. *After we have stopped thinking about the subject of our previous relationship, which once preoccupied our minds, we can allow God to restore all of the injured parts of our lives. God wants to give us new friends, new dates, and new ways of thinking. We can then say with the psalmist:*

Psalm 119:37
"Turn away my eyes from looking at vanity, and revive me in Thy ways."

It is very important to observe how we deal with the disappointment of being rejected by someone for whom we cared. When we learn to respond in the right way to rejection, we will be on our way to dynamic Christian living. It will bring glory to God when we can say after being dropped by the person closest to us:

Psalm 116:6-7
6) "The Lord preserves the simple; I was brought low and He saved me.
7) "Return to your rest, O my soul, for the Lord has dealt bountifully with you."

God's view of the misuse of

DRUGS AND ALCOHOL

Nothing has so swept the high school and college campuses of our country like the misuse of drugs and alcohol. Few of us need to be convinced that the problem is a growing phenomenon.

Most of us daily see evidence of drug and alcohol abuse at school or among people we know. Just about everyone has seen, at school or at a party, someone stagger by us drunk or "loaded."

We as Christians do not live in an isolated or protected world. It's easy for some of us to be attracted to the world of drugs and alcohol. Because this is true, some Christians are confused as to what God has to say on the subject and what their response should be to God's counsel on drugs and alcohol.

IN THIS CHAPTER LET'S STUDY TOGETHER...

- *What God says about drugs and alcohol.*
- *Why God says what He says about drugs and alcohol.*
- *What our response should be to His commands.*

I. WHAT DOES GOD SAY ABOUT THE MISUSE OF DRUGS?

GOD IS AGAINST US BEING INTOXICATED FROM THE MISUSE OF ANY DRUG OR ALCOHOL

WHAT IS INTOXICATION?

Intoxication, commonly known as "under the influence," is the physical state where a person's brain functioning is altered so that the individual is no longer in complete control of his own actions. As for the Christian, he is no longer able to allow the Holy Spirit complete control of his life, since his reasoning process is altered and he is unable to think and act logically.

> *GOD IS VERY CLEAR ON THE SUBJECT OF DRUGS AND ALCOHOL.*
> *Since the misuse of drugs and alcohol is so devastating,*
> *God in no way wants us to be confused about our use of it.*

Throughout Scripture, God continually refers to His negative feelings about getting "drunk" or"loaded" with either drugs or alcohol.

Proverbs 20:1
"Wine is a mocker, strong drink a brawler, and whoever is intoxicated by it is not wise"(emphasis added).

* *Why do you think God calls wine a mocker and strong drink a brawler?* ______________________________

____

* *What does God have to say about the person who gets drunk or loaded?* ______________________________

____

God not only thinks getting intoxicated is foolish, but the Bible also indicates that He takes getting drunk personally.

Isaiah 5:11-12 (Living Bible)
11) "Woe to you who get up early in the morning to go on long drinking bouts that last till late at night--woe to you drunken bums.
12) "You furnish lovely music at your grand parties; the orchestras are superb! But for the Lord you have no thought or care."

If God were to speak in everday high school language, He might put it this way:

HIGH SCHOOL PARAPHRASE OF ISAIAH 5:11-12

"Bad news for you, drunkard, pothead, junkie, you get stoned before school begins and keep yourself high all day long lasting even late into the night. You make sure your parties are filled with the latest rock sounds, and yet your mind is so wasted you can't even begin to think of the greatness of God nor of all the good things He has done."

* *According to Isaiah 5:12, why is it that God takes intoxication by chemicals personally?* ______________________________________

____

God sees that the misuse of liquor and drugs is a big enemy of those who indulge in them.

In a very dramatic way God Himself states His case so that all can understand what He means when He says:

1 Corinthians 6:9-10
9) "Or do you not know that the unrighteous shall not inherit the kingdom of God? Do not be deceived; neither fornicators, nor idolaters, nor adulterers, nor effeminate, nor homosexuals,
10) "nor thieves, nor the covetous, nor drunkards, nor revilers, nor swindlers, shall inherit the kingdom of God" (emphasis added).

It is not difficult for us to comprehend that God is clearly against the misuse of drugs and alcohol.

God in no way wants His children to be involved in drinking or "pot" parties. But why? Why is it that God is so strongly against drunkenness or intoxication? Let's look more closely at why God says what He says about drugs and alcohol.

II. GOD THINKS THAT OUR PHYSICAL BODY IS VERY IMPORTANT AND HE DOES NOT WANT IT DAMAGED BY THE BAD EFFECTS OF DRUGS AND ALCOHOL.

God tells us in His Word that you and I are made in the image of God. He put work and creativity into making us. God is a healthy, whole Being, and He wants us to be that way as much as possible. When we destroy our bodies or emotions so that we cannot think or act as strongly as God intended, we go against God's purpose in creating us. This grieves God very much.

Here is a list of some of the negative effects drugs and alcohol have on our bodies. Note that with the misuse of alcohol and drugs come physical and emotional damage.

MARIJUANA

Physical Damage

- *Reduces reflexes*
- *Impairs judgment*
- *Causes distortion of distance and time*
- *Can cause chronic bronchitis*
- *Damages memory cells in the brain*

Emotional Damage

- *Creates a "sense of well being" even in the face of danger*
- *Distorts emotional perception so that long-term use can cause depression*
- *Alters reality -- making temporary escape from personal "hang ups" easy -- leads to despair*
- *Generally promotes a lower self-achievement level*
- *Emotional extremes from drowsiness to anxiety*

ALCOHOL

Physical Damage

- *Impairs liver functioning*
- *Destroys body cells*
- *Puts undue stress on heart*
- *Impairs memory, judgment, and learning*

Emotional Damage

- *Social embarrassment from improper actions*
- *Attempt to handle stress through drinking causes anxiety*
- *Causes family hassles*
- *Guilt from misbehavior*
- *Poor self-image*

PILLS (Stimulants-amphetamines; depressants-barbiturates)

Physical Damage

- Unable to sleep properly
- Unable to eat properly
- Physical addiction
- Withdrawal pains (nervousness, tremors, convulsions)

Emotional Damage

- Deep depression
- Produces hallucinations and delirium
- Paranoia ("Persecution complex")
- Argumentative, overactive, unusually talkative

To God, a Christian's body and physical condition are very important. He tells us in His Word that He not only owns our bodies but that He actually lives inside of them.

1 Corinthians 6:19-20 (Living Bible)
19) "Haven't you yet learned that your body is the home of the Holy Spirit God gave you, and that He lives within you? Your own body does not belong to you.
20) "For God has bought you with a great price. So use every part of your body to give glory back to God, because He owns it."

* According to I Corinthians 7:19-20, for whom does our body serve as a home? ______________________

* How important is our body to God? ______________________

____

* According to I Corinthians 7:19-20, what should we be doing with our bodies? ______________________

* Why should we be doing this with our bodies? ______________________

God lives in our bodies and wants to make them a place of holy worship. He is intent on removing all the garbage that gets into His way of making our bodies a habitation of holy worship. We will be frustrated, and God cannot pour out His richest blessings, when we block this cleansing job that God is doing by "junking up our bodies."

III. GOD IS AGAINST THE MISUSE OF DRUGS AND ALCOHOL BECAUSE WHEN A PERSON IS INTOXICATED IT IS IMPOSSIBLE FOR HIM TO SEEK GOD AND PRAISE HIM COHERENTLY.

God wants us to make it our life's goal and purpose to seek and praise Him. To seek and praise God involves a determined effort of our entire being. A clear mind is of extreme importance if we are to seek and praise God in the way He wants us to.

Therefore, God in His love wants us to have a sound and disciplined mind.

2 Timothy 1:7
"For God has not given us a spirit of timidity, but of power and love and discipline."

God asks us to be in an attitude of prayer at all times. The Bible tells us what condition our minds should be in when we pray.

1 Peter 4:7
(New International Version)
"The end of all things is near. Therefore be clear-minded and self-controlled so that you can pray" (emphasis added).

The obvious question worth asking is, Can a person have a mind to clearly seek and praise God when he or she is drunk or high?

* Can a person's mind be controlled by God and by drugs at the same time? ______________________________

God answers this question with an emphatic NO! He says:

Ephesians 5:18 (Living Bible)
"Don't drink too much wine, for many evils lie along that path; but be filled instead with the Holy Spirit and controlled by Him.

Here we see that God commands us to be under the influence, or control, of the Holy Spirit at all times - anything that interferes with this control is disobedience to God.

Any person who thinks that getting drunk or "loaded" is helping him or her get closer to God is only fooling himself.

Being drunk or "spaced out" only grieves the Holy Spirit, the very One who helps us to experience who God is.

IV. GOD IS TOTALLY AGAINST THE MISUSE OF DRUGS AND ALCOHOL BECAUSE HE SEES THE USE OF THEM AS A FUTILE ATTEMPT TO ESCAPE REALITY.

There are no doubt many reasons why people get drunk or "loaded." Some are bored and want to escape the monotony of boredom.

Others believe that if they get involved in this type of activity they will surely be accepted by their friends.

Still others are driven by a desire to find the mystical excitement or the supposed new strength that the chemical might bring.

But whatever the motive for taking drugs or drinking, it is clear that they are used as a psychological crutch to keep one from facing the real world.

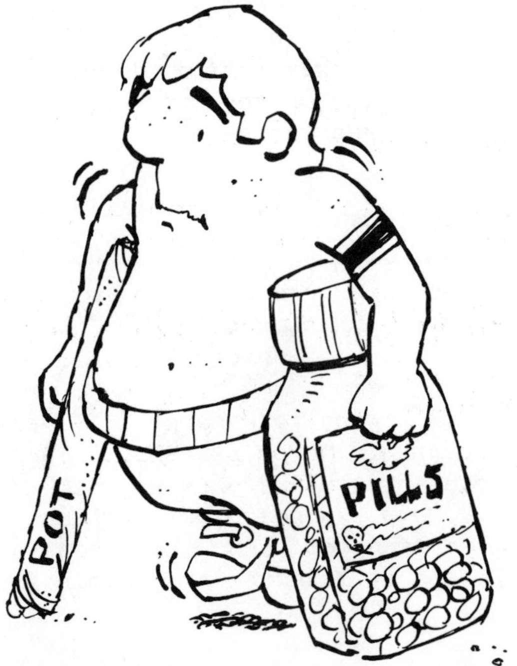

In the Old Testament, God describes through the prophet Isaiah some people who were not dealing with reality.

Isaiah 56:12 (Living Bible)
"'Come.' they say, 'We'll get some wine and have a party; let's all get drunk. This is really living; let it go on, and tomorrow will be better yet.'"

✱ *As you look at the passage (Isaiah 56:12), why do you believe these people were not living in the real world?* ____________

____

GOD IS A REALIST

He has never tried to escape from life as it really is.

When the awfulness of sin entered the world, God did not try to escape or distort what really took place. He dealt with the real life situation head on. He became man in the person of Jesus Christ and faced up to the awfulness of what was taking place. Jesus did not try to escape from the cross. Dying on the cross was neither easy nor an emotional high. He did not even have a drug to kill the physical pain.

Jesus Christ, the Son of God, our supreme Example, experienced joy and sorrow, pain and victory, and never once ran from the real world.

Supported by His power and love, God wants us as His children to see that dealing with reality rather than running from it is what it means to be living in the truth, and that's the only way to be truly happy.

The problem with trying to escape life's situations through a chemical is that the escape is never permanent. Sooner or later the real world and all its consequences catches up with us. So in the end, drugs or alcohol do not help us escape our problems and pressures -- they only complicate them even more. So that those who use intoxication as a way of escape end up like the tragic man in Proverbs 23.

Proverbs 23:29-35

29-30) "Who has woe? Who has sorrow? Who has contentions? Who has complaining? Who has wounds without cause? Who has redness of eyes? Those who linger long over wine, those who go to taste mixed wine.

31) "Do not look on the wine when it is red, when it sparkles in the cup, when it goes down smoothly;

32) "At the last it bites like a serpent, and stings like a viper.

33) "Your eyes will see strange things and your mind will utter perverse things.

34) "And you will be like one who lies down in the middle of the sea, or like one who lies down on the top of a mast.

35) "'They struck me, but I did not become ill; they beat me, but I did not know it. When shall I awake? I will seek another drink.'"

V. God is against the misuse of drugs and alcohol because it produces a counterfeit peace that hinders people from finding the true joy only God can give.

Satan is the greatest counterfeiter who has ever lived. It is his goal to offer a synthetic version of what only God can give. Satan deceives people into thinking that drugs and alcohol can give them the happiness and peace that only God can produce. But in reality, Satan can't even begin to offer the joy and peace that comes through knowing Jesus Christ.

A. JESUS OFFERS A QUALITY OF LIFE THAT IS FULL OF PEACE

Jesus has given all true believers in Him a tremendous promise. He said:

John 14:27 (Living Bible)
"I am leaving you with a gift - peace of mind and heart! And the peace I give isn't fragile like the peace the world gives. So don't be troubled or afraid."

According to this Bible passage, what is different about Christ's gift of peace? ______________________________

____

There is something that is really fantastic about Christ's peace when He comes to live within us. This peace is not always a great ecstatic high, but with it comes a deep mellow sense of purposeful meaning and joy that is unquenchable, despite whatever circumstances may surround us. Those who truly seek after Christ experience a sense of purpose and joy so great that no person can completely comprehend it.

B. JESUS OFFERS A QUALITY OF LIFE THAT IS STABLE

God spoke through the prophet Isaiah to us about the stabilizing, "together" influence He wants to have in our lives.

Isaiah 40:29-31
29) "He gives strength to the weary, and to him who lacks might He increases power.
30) "Though youths grow weary and tired, and vigorous young men stumble badly,
31) "Yet those who wait for the Lord will gain new strength; they will mount up with wings like eagles, they will run and not get tired, they will walk and not become weary."

* *What happens to those who chose to find their stability and strength ("togetherness") in something other than the Lord?* _____

____

* *According to the above verses what will happen to those who rest in the Lord?* ____

There is nothing stable about the misuse of mind-altering chemicals. In time they only bring guilt, disillusion, and confusion.

* *Can you think of ways that drugs and alchol bring confusion?*

____

____

____

____

____

____

____

____

____

____

God is always at work to bring our life into focus. The Bible talks about this:

1 Corinthians 14:33
"For God is not a God of confusion but of peace, as in all the churches of the saints."

True "togetherness" does not come from drinking hard liquor or being a "pothead." It comes from the stability that only God can give. If you want to get your life together - TRY GOD.

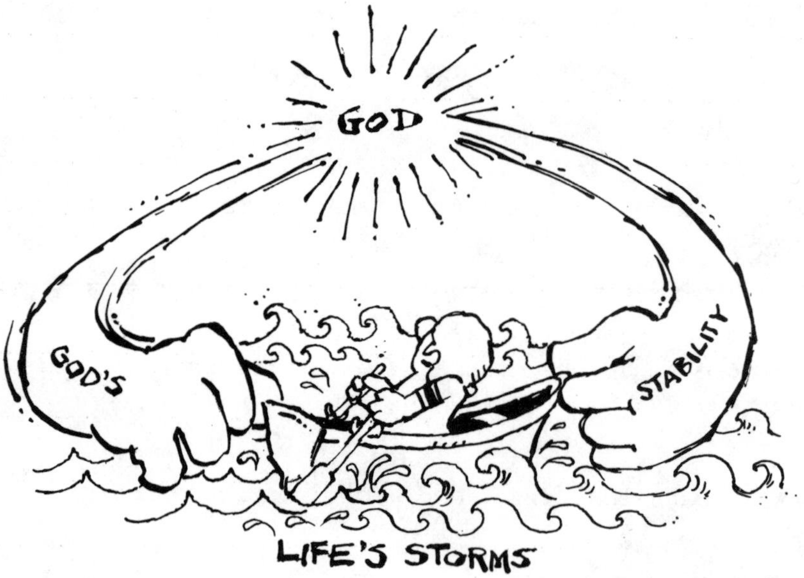

C. JESUS OFFERS A QUALITY OF LIFE THAT IS FULL OF LOVE

Every person who has ever tried drugs or gotten drunk is seeking love. Some turn to alcohol and pills to try to fill the emptiness of not finding real love in their lives. Drugs and alcohol cannot love or do loving things for the user.

Because

Love builds a person up, and the misuse of chemicals only brings him down.

PROJECT

EXPLAIN HOW YOU THINK DRUGS AND ALCOHOL ARE NOT LOVING

God's quality of life, however, is filled with love. God's love is not simply better than drugs but better than life itself. King David spoke of this in:

Psalm 63:3
"Because Thy lovingkindness is better than life, my lips will praise Thee."

God's love for us is so great that He chose to die for us. Drugs and alcohol cause people to die - but never do the people behind them ever die for anyone. But the Bible says:

Romans 5:8
"But God demonstrates His own love toward us, in that while we were yet sinners, Christ died for us."

Project

MAKE A LIST OF REASONS WHY GOD'S LOVE IS SO MUCH BETTER THAN ANYTHING DRUGS CAN GIVE YOU

IT IS OBVIOUS THAT THE LOVE THAT GOD BRINGS US IS BY FAR SUPERIOR TO ANY HIGH THAT CHEMICALS CAN BRING.

D. The Quality of Life That Jesus Gives Gets Better and Better as Time Passes

The sad thing about most drugs and alcohol is that one has to take more of the chemical all the time to attain the original high.

But after a while the high obtained can no longer completely satisfy the needs of the user.

So the user is ultimately wanting more but getting less. It is a fruitless vicious circle.

BUT THIS IS THE WAY GOD WORKS!
God is in the business of satisfying those who come to Him to have their needs met, no matter what those needs may be.

How Does God Work It?

John 6:35
"Jesus said to them, 'I am the bread of life; he who comes to Me shall not hunger, and he who believes in Me shall never thirst.'"

Jesus taught that the answers to life are not in a drug but in Himself.

God has designed that, as we seek Him, He satisfies that longing desire.

As He satisfies that longing desire, He puts within us a yet deeper desire to know Him more. So the Christian is always longing in a deeper way--yet always being satisfied in a deeper way. That is why David could say:

Psalm 63:1-2
1) "O God, Thou art my God; I shall seek Thee earnestly; my soul thirsts for Thee, my flesh yearns for Thee, in a dry and weary land where there is no water.
2) "Thus I have beheld Thee in the sanctuary, to see Thy power and Thy glory."
And Jesus said:

Matthew 5:6
"Blessed are those who hunger and thirst for righteousness, for they shall be satisfied."

Trying to compare what drugs and alcohol offer with what God in Jesus Christ offers is like comparing a drop of water with the ocean--there is, in fact, no comparison.

The quality of life we have in Jesus Christ is one that is full of peace, stability, love and satisfaction, and it will get better and better for all eternity.

THERE IS NOTHING THAT CAN COMPARE TO THIS KIND OF LIFE.

WHAT OUR RESPONSE SHOULD BE TO GOD'S COMMAND

When confronted by drugs and alcohol, we need to behave as God's holy children.

Because of our sin nature, we can still be attracted to the garbage of this world. We sometimes think that the life-style we had before coming to Christ is more attractive and worth trying again. God doesn't want us to be fooled by such doubtful thinking.

God says:

Romans 13:13-14 (Living Bible)
13) "Be decent and true in everything you do so that all can approve your behavior. Don't spend your time in wild parties and getting drunk or in adultery and lust, or fighting, or jealousy.
14) "But ask the Lord Jesus Christ to help you live as you should, and don't make plans to enjoy evil."

* *According to the above passage, what are some reasons we should be true and decent?* ______________________________

____

We should live as Christ lived.

1 John 2:6
"The one who says he abides in Him ought himself to walk in the same manner as He walked."

Jesus did not walk around on this earth drunk or "loaded." He taught and lived a life that proved He was One with the Father.

Since Christ lives in us, and our bodies house His Spirit -- we need to do the same.

We Need Compassion

We need to look at people involved in drugs and alcohol with a real spirit of compassion.

It is easy for us to become insensitive and cruel to those who are enslaved by the awfulness of drugs and alcohol. Jesus does not want us to look down our noses at these people but to help them out of their vicious circle.

What a privilege for us to be the very vessel in which Christ lives. How important it is for us to protect this temple and not junk it up with drugs and alcohol.

1 Thessalonians 5:7-9
7) "For those who sleep, do their sleeping at night, and those who get drunk, get drunk at night.
8) "But since we are of the day, let us be sober, having put on the breastplate of faith and love, and as a helmet, the hope of salvation.
9) "For God has not destined us for wrath, but for obtaining salvation through our Lord Jesus Christ."

NOTES

How to break

BAD HABITS

Every one of us has habits; habits do not have to be bad. Some are very good and helpful. For example, do you:

- *Put on your left or your right shoe first?*
- *Put your pants or your shoes on first?*
- *Turn the shower on before or after you get in it?*
- *Tie your shoe by wrapping the laces forward or backward?*

Most of us do not stop and think when we do these activities--they have become automatic. They are habits! They are helpful habits to us because we can accomplish tasks more rapidly, and that frees us to be thinking about something else at the same time.

Yet, there are some activities, which we do over and over again, that are harmful to us and displeasing to God--these are called "bad habits."

Definition of a bad habit: Any thought or action that becomes involuntary or compulsive through frequent repetition is displeasing to a holy God.

Needless to say, God wants us to get rid of those activities that we do repeatedly that dismay, anger, and hurt God.

SINCE THE BREAKING OF BAD HABITS IS SO IMPORTANT, LET'S STUDY TOGETHER..
WHAT CAUSES A BAD HABIT?
STEPS TO BREAKING A BAD HABIT

I. WHAT CAUSES A BAD HABIT?

An evil or harmful habit is caused by repeatedly giving in to the impulses of our rebellious sin nature. The more we yield to the wrong habit, the more this bad habit becomes ingrained into our life-styles. The Bible teaches that each of us has a sin nature, which is a very powerful motivating drive within us and is opposed to God. This sin nature is often referred to in Scripture as "the flesh."

Our sin nature is fighting with the Spirit of God for the control of our will.

Galatians 5:17 (Living Bible)
"For we naturally love to do evil things that are just the opposite from the things that the Holy Spirit tells us to do; and the good things we want to do when the Spirit has his way with us are just the opposite of our natural desires. These two forces within us are constantly fighting each other to win control over us, and our wishes are never free from their pressures."

Repeated carrying through on wrong decisions will lead to our becoming enslaved to sin. This is the desire of both Satan and our own sin nature.

The Bible talks about this enslavement in:

Romans 6:16 (Living Bible)
"Don't you realize that you can choose your own master? You can choose sin (with death) or else obedience (with life). The one to whom you offer yourself--he will take you and be your master and you will be his slave."

*According to the above passage, is it possible to become a slave of sin in our habits? ______________________________

____

THE FLESH IS THE CULPRIT

We have come to see that bad habits spring out of our flesh, or our own sin nature. It is the plan of our flesh to get us to obey its impulses to sin. If our sin nature can get us to disobey God and His ways enough times, then it will have us in bondage to our bad habits. This bondage fulfills Satan's desire to discourage and defeat each Christian by establishing us in activities that do not please God.

PROJECT

FINDING YOUR BAD HABITS

Here is a list of some of the bad habits people have. Go over the list and pick out which ones plague your life.

____*I smoke (1 Corinthians 6:12, 18-20).*

____*I do drugs a little (1 Corinthians 6:12, 18-20).*

____*I drink wine, beer, or hard liquor (1 Corinthians 6:12, 18-20).*

____*I eat too much or snack between meals (1 Corinthians 6:12, 18-20; Galatians 5*

____*I blame others when things go wrong (Ephesians 4:29; Philippians 2:3-4).*

____*I am slow to admit I am wrong and I argue a lot (Philippians 2:2-5).*

____*I drive over the speed limit (Romans 13:1-5).*

____*I bite my nails 1 Corinthians 6:19-20; Philippians 4:6-7; 1 Peter 5:7).*

____*My temper flares up whenever things don't go right (Proverbs 16:32; Ecclesiastes 7:9; Matthew 5:22-24; Ephesians 4:31-32; James 1:19-20).*

____*I make sarcastic and cutting remarks (Ephesians 4:29; James 3:6).*

____*I buy things impulsively, without thinking it through (Matthew 6:31-33; 1 Corinthians 4:2; 1 Timothy 6:10-11).*

____*I waste too much time daydreaming (Proverbs 23:6-7; 2 Corinthians 10:3-5).*

____*I have trouble getting up in the morning (Proverbs 6:6-11; 24:33-34).*

____*I avoid new people and new situations (Romans 13:8; 8:28; Philippians 4:6-7; 1 Peter 2:16-17).*

____*I read unhealthy and worthless books and magazines (Matthew 5:27-28; 6:33; 2 Corinthians 10:3-5; 1 Thessalonians 4:3-4).*

____*I talk too much about the opposite sex (Matthew 12:34-37; 15:18-20; Ephesians 4:29; 1 Peter 5:7).*

____*I am noisy and obnoxious (Ecclesiastes 9:17; Romans 14:19; Ephesians 4:29; Philippians 2:3-4; 1 Thessalonians 4:11).*

____*I clown around whenever serious topics are discussed (Ephesians 4:29; 5:4; Philippians 2:3-4).*

____*I talk too much about myself (1 Corinthians 13:4-8; Galatians 6:2-3; Ephesians 4:29; Philippians 2:3-4).*

____*It is easy for me to lie my way out of a tough situation (Exodus 20:16; Ephesians 4:25, 29; Colossians 3:9).*

____*I boast and exaggerate to make myself look better (Luke 22:26-27; Ephesians 4:25, 29; 1 Peter 5:6).*

____*I enjoy repeating negative information that I have heard about others (Romans 1:29; Ephesians 4:25, 29).*

____*I quickly scream or throw things when something goes wrong (Proverbs 16:32; Ephesians 4:31-32; James 1:19-20).*

____*I spend too much time in front of the mirror (Matthew 6:25; 1 John 2:15-17).*

____*My room, locker, or personal belongings are sloppy (1 Corinthians 10:31; 14:33, 40).*

____*I can't stop masturbating (Matthew 5:27-28; 1 Corinthians 6:18-20; 2 Corinthians 10:3-5; 1 Thessalonians 4:3-4).*

____*I flirt to get attention, admiration, or just to have my own way (Luke 22:26; James 4:10; 1 Peter 5:6).*

____*I put off doing things I should get done (devotions, homework, etc.) (Matthew 6:33-34; 25:24-30; 1 Corinthians 4:2; Ephesians 5:12, 16).*

____*I worry about things over which I have little control (Matthew 6:25-34; Philippians 4:6-7; 1 Peter 5:7).*

____*I swear a lot (James 3:9-10).*

____*I waste too much time watching TV (Romans 12:1-2; 1 Corinthians 4:2; 2 Corinthians 10:3-5; Ephesians 5:3).*

II. Steps to Take in Breaking a Bad Habit

We know what a bad habit is and how our sinful nature wars against us to defeat us. But that knowledge, by itself, may not help us to break a defeated life-style. God, in His Word, gives us some practical help on how to be freed from bad habits.

A. To Break a Bad Habit, We Must Be Serious About Quitting

No one breaks a bad habit unless he really wants to. It is easy to look at some of the negative practices we have and fool ourselves into thinking that our enslaving habits are not that damaging. That type of reasoning comes only from our own deceitful sin nature, which resists any kind of change for the better.

Jeremiah 17:9
"The heart is more deceitful than all else and is desperately sick; who can understand it?"

1. Habits are Serious Because God Thinks They are Serious

In the Sermon on the Mount, Jesus was talking about the sinful habit of lusting after women. His instruction on that occasion demonstrates that He does not take sin habits lightly and that He expects us to do something about them.

Matthew 5:29-30
29) "And if your right eye makes you stumble, tear it out, and throw it from you; for it is better for you that one of the parts of your body perish, than for your whole body to be thrown into hell.
30) "And if your right hand makes you stumble, cut if off, and throw it from you; for it is better for you that one of the parts of your body perish, than for your whole body go into hell."

It should be obvious to us that Jesus was not teaching that we should mutilate our bodies. Neither will a Christian lose his salvation if he lusts.

Rather, the main teaching of this passage is that sin is amazingly destructive and must be dealt with in a powerful way. We must take definite action against our wrong habits if we are to see victory. We cannot simply ignore these unwelcome practices and hope they will go away--they won't!

2. Bad Habits are Serious Because They Have Already Kept Us From Fulfilling Our Greatest Potential for God.

God has more things planned for our lives than we could ever think possible. Most of us have only begun to live out our great potential for God. Paul wrote to a young man, Timothy, that God wants each Christian to be available for His use at every moment. We should allow no addiction to a pet sin to keep us from this place of service.

2 Timothy 2:21: "Therefore, if a man cleanses himself from these things, he will be a vessel for honor, sanctified, useful to the Master, prepared for every good work."

According to 2 Timothy 2:21, what must a man be willing to do if he is desperate enough to stop doing bad habits? _________

____

Hebrews 12:1 (Living Bible)
"Since we have such a huge crowd of men of faith watching us from the grandstands, let us strip off anything that slows us down or holds us back, and especially those sins that wrap themselves so tightly around our feet and trip us up; and let us run with patience the particular race that God has set before us."

In this verse we have a description of what our bad habits do to us as we try to live for Christ.

According to the verse Hebrews 12:1, what are the effects of our sinful habits on our Christian walk? ____________________

____

It is evident from Scripture that God wants us to think about where we could be for God today, if our bad habits had been broken.

PROJECT

Refer again to the list of bad habits listed on pages 78 and 79. Consider each one of your five worst habits.

WRITE OUT A PARAGRAPH ON EACH ONE DESCRIBING HOW YOUR LIFE WOULD BE MORE DYNAMIC FOR CHRIST TODAY IF YOU HAD NEVER HAD THESE HABITS.

It should now be obvious why God thinks breaking bad habits is serious business.

3. Bad Habits Are Serious Because of the Trouble They Will Lead to in the Future

Sin,
if it is not stopped,
will always lead to greater and more disasterous evil.
God sees our lives, not only today, abut also in the future.
If we are gripped by a habit now, how much more powerfully will it affect other areas of our lives in the years to come? God talks about the future results of our wrong habits:

Galatians 6:7-8 (Living Bible)
7) "Don't be misled; remember that you can't ignore God and get away with it: a man will always reap just the kind of crop he sows!
8) "If he sows to please his own wrong desires, he will be planting seeds of evil and he will surely reap a harvest of spiritual decay and death; but if he plants the good things of the Spirit, he will reap the everlasting life which the Holy Spirit gives him."

* *What do these verses teach that a man does that will lead to his own spiritual decay and death?* ______________________

____

Some people think that their habit is not that powerful nor will it affect their life in the future. You will hear them say, "I can quit any time I want to." Little do they know that daily their habit is getting stronger and will become a mean tyrant having devastating effects.

ILLUSTRATION PROJECT

Consider the following illustration. Take a spool of thread. Wrap one strand around the fingers of your hand. No doubt it will be easy to break. Now wrap the thread around your fingers 15 more times, and try to break free. You will find this much more difficult, if not impossible. The thread itself is no stronger, but the repeated winding of the thread will prevent it from being broken. In much the same way, the repeated acting out of a sin's impulse will soon lead to bondage for the rest of your life.

PROJECT

WHAT COULD HAPPEN IN 15 YEARS

List again your 5 worst habits from the list on pages 78 and 79. If these habits are not stopped during the next 15 years, but in fact get worse and more deeply ingrained in your life, describe some of the results of each of these in the following areas:

Your marriage
Your work
Your walk with God.

B. To Break a Bad Habit, We Must Know What We are Going to Do About It.

THERE MUST BE AN ACT OF OUR WILL, A COMMITMENT TO GOD.

Some may still think that they can enjoy their habit and also maintain a rich and peaceful Christian life. The Bible calls this kind of person a "double-minded man, unstable in all his ways." A double-minded man is undecided between two choices. Sometimes he chooses for God's way and sometimes for the impulses of his sin nature.

Because of his indecision he is unpredictable and untrustworthy as far as God is concerned. His life is a series of ups and downs, victories and defeats, joys and frustrations. God in no way wants us to be wishy-washy in our commitment to follow and obey Him. He wants us to have one mind and follow wholeheartedly, whatever our plan of action is to be. God knows that double-minded thinking is futile.

In Luke 16:13, Jesus talks about a man who had the habit of seeing money as the cure for all his needs. Evidently, this man believed that he needed to worship God too. But Jesus explained the impossiblity of double thinking.

Luke 16:13
"No servant can serve two masters; for either he will hate the one, and love the other, or else he will hold to one, and despise the other. You cannot serve God and mammon [money]."

☆ THINK BACK FOR A MOMENT . . .

* *Think of a time when you were deeply involved in a sinful habit.*

  At the actual time of experiencing that sin, what were your thoughts about God? ______________________________

  ____

If we are honest with ourselves, we would probably have to admit that He was not in our minds at all or that we were consciously trying to block Him out of our thinking.

* *Think of a time when you were most excited about Jesus Christ.*

  During that time, what were your thoughts about your sin habits?

  ____

  ____

It is God's will that we decide who we will obey and then commit ourselves totally to follow that master with our whole being.

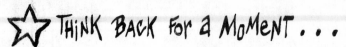

There was a church in the New Testament that couldn't decide whether to follow God or to obey her sin impulses. So the church tried to do a little of both. Jesus set the church straight on the matter. He said:

Revelation 3:15-16
15) "I know your deeds, that you are neither cold nor hot; I would that you were cold or hot.
16) "So because you are lukewarm, and neither hot nor cold, I will spit you out of my mouth."

Jesus actually gets sick over those of us who think that we can have two minds.

God wants His followers to develop a will that is determined to obey God no matter what the feelings or circumstances.

THE GREATEST COMPLIMENT THAT WE CAN PAY TO GOD IS:

to say with our will, "I want to obey You because of who You are, in spite of the immediate circumstances or my emotions at the moment."

There is no greater example of determination to obey God than the life of Jesus Christ Himself. He had one mind; a mind firmly set on doing the Father's will, no matter what the cost. He spoke of this attitude of total obedience:

John 14:31 (Living Bible)
"...I will freely do what the Father requires of me so that the world will know that I love the Father."

* *What did Jesus prove to the world when he obeyed God with his total will?* ____

____

Jesus did not simply talk in easy-to-say generalities. He lived what He taught in rough-and-tumble everyday life.

THE BIG TEST OF CHRISTIAN COMMITMENT

There was nothing more difficult in Christ's life on earth than His going through the experience of the cross. His body and emotions recoiled from going through such an ugly event. But Jesus was determined. He had set his whole mind on doing the Father's will--no matter how difficult. The prophet Isaiah spoke of Christ's determination hundreds of years before Christ went to the Garden of Gethsemane and then on to the cross.

Isaiah 50:5-7
5) "The Lord God has opened My ear; and I was not disobedient, nor did I turn back.
6) "I gave My back to those who strike me, and My cheeks to those who pluck out the beard; I did not cover My face from humiliation and spitting.
7) "For the Lord God helps Me, therefore, I am not disgraced; therefore, I have set my face like flint, and I know that I shall not be ashamed."

In the Garden of Gethsemane, all of Christ's emotions pulled at His will. They screamed at Him to leave the Garden and not go through the awful ordeal of suffering and shame. But Christ's will stood against the emotions and circumstances of that moment. He did not waver from doing God's will, yet that great conflict caused Christ to sweat great drops of blood during the battle.

We too face battles against the old sin nature and its habits. God wants our wills to be so strong that we, too, would be willing to sweat great drops of blood in our struggle to obey God and shun sin.

Hebrews 12:3-4
3) "For consider Him who has endured such hostility by sinners against Himself, so that you may not grow weary and lose heart.
4) "You have not yet resisted to the point of shedding blood in your striving against sin."

CAN YOU SAY, "I am determined to serve God because of His greatness, no matter what my feelings say to oppose me?"

I Will serve God Because He is . . . ______________________________

____

____

____

____

____

To Break a Bad Habit, We Must Realize

Realize that in God's power, we don't have to continue doing our destructive habits.

Many people have just about given up in their struggle against sin. They have come to view their sin nature as some tireless evil taskmaster whom they are helpless to resist. So they rationalize sinful habits as though there is nothing that can be done to stop them.

God wants us to know not only that victory over our sin nature is possible, but also that we are in fact, through faith in Christ, dead to its impulses to do wrong.

Because of Christ's death and resurrection, our sin nature has lost its power to make us perform sinful habits.

The Bible talks about this:

Romans 6:2,3,6,7 (Living Bible)

2,3) "...Should we keep on sinning when we don't have to? For sin's power over us was broken when we became Christians and were baptized to become a part of Jesus Christ; through his death the power of your sinful nature was shattered.

6) "Your old evil desires were nailed to the cross with him; that part of you that loves to sin was crushed and fatally wounded, so that your sin-loving body is no longer under sin's control, no longer needs to be a slave to sin;

7) "for when you are deadened to sin you are freed from all its allure and its power over you."

*According to Romans 6:3, what amazing statement does God make about true Christians? ____________________

____

*What phrases in the passages Romans 6:2-3, 6-7 state what Christ did to our sin nature at the cross? ____________________

____

*What quality of life is now available to us, since Christ fatally wounded our sin nature, according to Romans 6:2-3, 6-7? ____

____

GOD SAYS A HEAVY !

In Romans, chapter 6, God says something fantastic about what has happened to our sin nature. God assures us that when Jesus Christ died on the cross, He took our old rebellious selves with Him. In this mysterious happening, God shattered the power of our evil selves to have influence over us. So then, we no longer have to be enslaved to our sin nature. We can be freed to live the Christian life as it is meant to be lived--IN THE POWER OF GOD.

BUT WE ASK . . .

* IF MY SIN NATURE HAS BEEN CRUSHED. . .
* IF IT IS POWERLESS TO CONTROL MY LIFE . . .
* IF MY OLD DESIRES WERE NAILED TO THE CROSS . . .
* IF THAT PART OF ME THAT WANTS TO SIN WAS FATALLY WOUNDED...

WHY ??

THEN AM I OFTEN DRIVEN BY THAT VERY SIN NATURE

THAT GOD SAYS IS DEAD ???

Our sin nature cannot make us perform bad habits when we live by faith, believing we are dead to its power.

It is difficult for us to accept what God says about our sin nature being dead, because we daily experience its impulses to do wrong. Yet, faith (believing God, purely as an act of our will) makes it possible for God's truth to become actual reality. Satan would like us to believe that just the opposite of what God says is true. He leads us to think that our sin nature is still our boss and that we are slaves to its commands.

That is why we must live as if what God says is true, no matter what the circumstances may say to the contrary.

Paul goes on to say this:

Romans 6:11-13 (Living Bible)
11) "So look upon your old sin nature as dead and unresponsive to sin, and instead be alive to God, alert to Him, through Jesus Christ our Lord.
12) "Do not let sin control your puny body any longer; do not give in to its sinful desires.
13) "Do not let any part of your bodies become tools of wickedness, to be used for sinning; but give yourselves completely to God--every part of you--for you are back from death and you want to be tools in the hands of God, to be used for his good purposes."

* *According to the above verses, what action must we take, believing what God says about the death of our sin nature?*

CHRIST PUT TO DEATH OUR EVIL SELF

SO WE CAN HAVE THE VICTORY.

Here are some practical steps that we can take to help us appropriate what God says about the death of our sin nature. These steps will help us when we are tempted to indulge in bad habits.

- *PICTURE IN YOUR MIND CHRIST DYING ON THE CROSS.*
- *AS BEST YOU CAN, VISUALIZE YOUR OWN SIN NATURE BEING CRUSHED AND PUT TO DEATH, WITH CHRIST, ON THE CROSS.*
- *PICTURE THE RISEN CHRIST STANDING OVER YOUR DEAD SIN NATURE AS ITS CONQUEROR.*
- *WITH THESE IMAGES IN MIND, SPEAK TO YOUR OLD SIN NATURE AND SAY, "I NO LONGER <u>HAVE TO</u> LISTEN TO YOU. <u>YOU ARE DEAD</u>!"*
- *LIST THE MEMBERS OF YOUR BODY WHICH WOULD HAVE BEEN INVOLVED IN THE SIN HABIT. GIVE THESE OVER TO CHRIST AS INSTRUMENTS TO BE USED IN HIS SERVICE.*
- *ASK GOD TO GUIDE YOUR THINKING AS YOU CREATIVELY DESIGN A SPECIFIC ACTIVITY FOR THESE SURRENDERED MEMBERS IN HIS SERVICE.*

It is God's will that we overcome our bad habits. And because of this desire, He has given us ways to avoid falling into them. We must remember that Christ put our sinful nature to death, and we can be successful in overcoming any bad habit. Our belief in God's ability to overcome our sinful nature, and acting on this belief, makes us able to thank Him and give ourselves completely to Him and to His service.

D. IN ORDER TO BREAK SOME BAD HABITS, GOD WANTS US TO RUN FROM OR RESIST THE CIRCUMSTANCES THAT CAUSE THE BAD HABITS.

Where do bad habits come from?

Almost every habit has a circumstance or an object that allows a bad habit to start and continue. In many cases, if these circumstances or objects were not accessible to the person, the habit would begin to disappear.

For example: if a person with a smoking habit could no longer get to cigarettes, his habit would soon begin to disappear. If a person with a habit of wasting time watching TV gave his TV away, he would eliminate the source of the bad habit.

God expects us to do the best we know--to stay away from circumstances or objects that feed our habits.

He makes His point very clear:
Romans 13:14
"But put on the Lord Jesus Christ, and make no provision for the flesh in regard to its lusts" (emphasis added).

Romans 13:14 (Living Bible)
"But ask the Lord Jesus Christ to help you live as you should and don't make plans to enjoy evil" (emphasis added).

* *What do you think the Bible means when it says, "Make no provision for the flesh in regard to its lusts"?* ____________

____

In the book of Proverbs, King Solomon was instructing his son about immoral, godless women. He said:

Proverbs 5:7-9
7) "Now then, my sons, listen to me, and do not depart from the words of my mouth.
8) "Keep your way far from her, and do not go near the door of her house,
9) "Lest you give your vigor to others and your years to the cruel one" (emphasis added).

* *What did Solomon want his son to do in order to avoid a rowdy woman sin problem?* ____

____

King Solomon knew his sons could plan their lives so that they could avoid becoming involved with immoral women.

Sometimes Satan and his demonic helpers arrange for us to come upon objects that lead to bad habits--when this happens God's command for us is to flee.

2 Timothy 2:22
"Now flee from youthful lusts, and pursue righteousness, faith, love and peace, with those who call on the Lord from a pure heart."

* *Why do you think God wants us to flee temptations?* ____________

____

____

NOT ALL HABITS CAN BE BROKEN BY AVOIDING OR RUNNING FROM THE CIRCUMSTANCES OR OBJECTS THAT FEED OUR BAD HABITS

Some habits we need to run from, but others we need to defeat by resisting the thoughts and actions that have led us to the grip of the habit.

God tells us what to do when Satan works in our minds to develop sin patterns in our lives.

James 4:7
"Submit therefore to God. Resist the devil and he will flee from you."

According to James 4:7, what two actions should we take when we are tempted? ______________________________

____

God tells us what to do when we are tempted by something we cannot avoid.

Ephesians 6:11-13
11) "Put on the full armor of God, that you may be able to stand firm against the schemes of the devil.
12) "For our struggle is not against flesh and blood, but against the rulers, against the powers, against the world forces of this darkness, against the spiritual forces of wickedness in the heavenly places.
13) "Therefore, take up the full armor of God, that you may be able to resist in the evil day, and having done everything, to stand firm."

According to Ephesians 6:11, 12, 13 what are we to do when we come up against a sin or temptation that we cannot flee? ____

____

____

____

Project

Go back over the list of habits on pages 77 and 78. Which habits are impossible to escape (physically)?

HOW DO WE RESIST SATAN, OR A TEMPTATION FROM WHICH WE CANNOT FLEE

* DRAW NEAR TO GOD — APPROPRIATE THE POWER OF THE HOLY SPIRIT

God must fill your heart and mind at a time like this. Ask Him to fill you with His Holy Spirit.

James 4:8-9
8) "Draw near to God and He will draw near to you. Cleanse your hands, you sinners; and purify your hearts, you double-minded.
9) "Be miserable and mourn and weep; let your laughter be turned into mourning, and your joy to gloom."

Ephesians 5:18
"But be filled with the Spirit."

* REALIZE WE HAVE NO AUTHORITY IN OURSELF AND CLAIM OUR AUTHORITY AS A BELIEVER IN CHRIST

We, in and of ourselves, are no match for Satan. He is much too deceitful and powerful, but with Christ in us we have tremendous authority to resist Satan and force him to leave.

1 John 4:4
"You are from God, little children, and have overcome them; because greater is He who is in you than he who is in the world."

* CLAIM THE BLOOD OF CHRIST

The thing that causes Satan and his demonic forces to run is the great work of Christ at the cross. Claim for yourself what Jesus has done for you at the cross.

Revelation 12:11
"And they overcame him because of the blood of the Lamb and because of the word of their testimony..."

* QUOTE SCRIPTURE

When you talk to evil forces or Satan himself, make sure you quote Scripture to them. Satan has no answer for the power of the Word.

John 15:7
"If you abide in Me, and My words abide in you, ask whatever you wish, and it shall be done for you."

* By Faith Believe What God Has Promised

God says that we can have victory over Satan inspired attacks. Faith in His promises will render the Evil One powerless.

1 John 5:14
"And this is the confidence which we have before Him, that, if we ask anything according to His will, He hears us."

Here is a Prayer You Pray When Resisting Satan

Dear Father, Thank you I can draw near to you. I thank you that I can now be filled with your Holy Spirit. By faith I believe this. I realize that I can do nothing by myself so I am claiming the authority of Jesus Christ, who lives inside of me. I claim your promise that the blood of Christ can give me power over sin. Father, I thank you that I can resist Satan and his demonic helpers and he will flee because Jesus lives in me and is greater than the Devil and all his forces. And by faith I believe that you are allowing me to resist this temptation and it is causing Satan and his forces to flee. In Jesus Name, Amen.

IN CONCLUSION

Breaking bad habits is never an easy thing to do. They are all around us as a result of wherever we go, whatever we see, whatever we do. But no matter how awful they seem, or how hard we think it will be to break them, all we have to do is think of Jesus Christ. How can He help us? What can He do that will put this habit away forever? God gives us clear instructions on how we can call on Him in time of need.

Before God can do anything, we have to want His help. We have to want to get rid of the habit--God will not help if in the back of our minds we enjoy what we are doing. We must realize that this is a sin in God's eyes and the only way it can be overcome is to take the problem to Him. Once we have come to this realization, nothing can stop Him from taking that bad habit out of your life. If God is in control, Satan hasn't got a chance to tempt you. He will flee from you because God is there. Because of this fact, we can rest peacefully in God's love and understanding.

God <u>wants</u> to help us. He's waiting for us to ask Him! God will never let you down--He will always succeed in destroying what Satan has put in our hearts and minds. God is assuredly stronger than Satan.

Let God show you how strong and powerful He is! He will win and will make you a winner over Satan. How exciting that can be! You'll be a new person in Christ--the bad habit washed away--conquered and totally destroyed.

It is God's desire that we come to Him with our problems. Why don't you ask Him and see what He can do for you?

NOTES

How to start
NEW HEALTHY HABITS

All true Christians want to form new healthy habits. God Himself wants you to form habits that are pleasing to Him. Jesus Christ had a life-style that was saturated with perfect habits. For example, it was Jesus' habit to go to the synagogue (Luke 4:16) and He also made it a habit to pray (John 6:15). Forming new Christ-like habits is not an easy thing to do.

Our sin nature, Satan, and the whole world system will fight us as we attempt to start a whole new habitual way of living. Yet, in spite of all the opposition that is against us to form new habits, God promises us success in His power for this important task. Not only does God want to supply this power, but He also tells us that it is important for us to discipline ourselves to form new healthy habits.

1 Timothy 4:7-8
7) "...discipline yourself for the purpose of godliness;
8) "for bodily discipline is only of little profit, but godliness is profitable for all things, since it holds promise for the present life and also for the life to come."

Let us discuss together <u>a plan that we can follow that will guarantee us success from God in forming new healthy habits</u>.

I. GOD'S PLAN FOR US TO FORM NEW HEALTHY HABITS IS FOR US TO PRAY

It is hard to form healthy new habits. <u>It is so difficult to form good new habits that we should not even attempt to do it in our own strength</u>. If we do try to form new habits in our own power we will only end up proud or frustrated and defeated. The kind of help that we need to form God's new habits in our lives comes only from God. Because this is true, we need to pray and ask for God's help in a very special way.

A. As we pray to God for help in forming new habits, we should first confess our sin.

Most of us already have formed a bad habit that we are doing instead of the healthy habit we want to do.

PROJECT

For example: **INSTEAD OF**

NEGATIVE	POSITIVE
We over-sleep	*Having a quiet time with God*
We buy impulsively	*Budgeting our money*
We make fun of people or say cruel things about them	*Building other people up*
We tend to worry	*Trusting God in a situation*

Usually, when we come to God about this problem of having too many bad habits and not enough good habits we are already dwelling on the negative habits because of our guilt feelings. But when we confess our bad habit to God and believe that He has totally removed our guilt from us, we free ourselves of the emotional grip of guilt. This freedom from guilt enables us to concentrate on Christ and allows us the time and energy to work on forming new meaningful habits.

We can have the freedom that David had when he prayed:

Psalm 32:1,2 (Living Bible)
"What happiness for those whose guilt has been forgiven! What joys when sins are covered over! What relief for those who have confessed their sins and God has cleared their record."

B. We Should Ask God to Give Us the Desire to Really Want to Form New Healthy Habits

Since we have such a warped sin nature at war within us, we need God to give us a whole new set of desires to be motivated to work on the new good habits.

King David, as he confessed his sin before God knew that he was going to have to be continually motivated by the Lord to live a life that was pleasing to God.

He prayed in:

Psalm 51:12
"Restore to me the joy of Thy salvation, and sustain me with a willing spirit."

It is not as though we have no desire at all to form a better life style. Most of the time, however, our desire to do good is not enough to see us through.

A man came to Jesus with a demon possessed son. He had faith that Jesus could heal his son, but the man's faith was not quite enough. The man made a profound statement to Jesus; He said:

Mark 9:24 (Living Bible)
"I do have faith, Oh help me to have more!"

We no doubt have a desire to start new good habits, but we need God's help to even have more of that yearning. In order to get the desire we must both ask and believe that God will give it.

C. WE SHOULD ASK GOD TO GIVE US THE POWER TO FORM NEW HEALTHY HABITS.

Where do we get the actual power to form habits that truly please God? God teaches us that this power comes in being controlled on a moment by moment basis by the Holy Spirit. God wants to give us His spirit of power that is so great it can do anything. That's what He said in:

2 Timothy 1:7
"For God has not given us a spirit of timidity, but of power and love and discipline."

Being controlled by the Holy Spirit is not a climatic once and for all experience but a continual work of God in our lives as we believe Him for it. God made this clear when He said in:

Galatians 5:16
"But I say, walk by the Spirit, and you will not carry out the desire of the flesh."

One way we know that we are walking in the Spirit is when we prayerfully ask God for His power through the Holy Spirit.

The Apostle Paul understood this when he wrote in:

Ephesians 3:14-16
14) "For this reason, I bow my knees before the Father,
15) "from whom every family in heaven and on earth derives its name,
16) "that He would grant you, according to the riches of His glory, to be strengthened with power through His Spirit in the inner man."

In order to begin forming new habits that please God, we must start by doing the very basic things right. We must begin by having meaningful, believing prayer. The prayers of confession and pleading for desire with power through the filling of the Holy Spirit are the prayers that will get results from God.

II. GOD'S PLAN FOR US TO BEGIN TO FORM NEW HEALTHY HABITS IS TO CLEAN UP OUR MINDS WITH A NEW WAY OF THINKING

The Bible indicates that we are greatly affected by what we think. Nothing has a greater impact on us than what our will--which is dictated by our minds--tells us to do. God put it so well in:

Proverbs 23:7
"For as he thinks within himself, so he is."

Jesus taught that all wrong comes flowing right out of our heart or our minds. He said in:

Mark 7:21-23
21) "For from within, out of the heart of men, proceed the evil thoughts and fornications, thefts, murders, adulteries,
22) "deeds of coveting and wickedness, as well as deceit, sensuality, envy, slander, pride and foolishness.
23) "All these evil things proceed from within and defile the man."

Project

Here is a list of bad habits. Can you find which of these habits really start with and are dictated by the mind?

- *I smoke*
- *I do drugs a little*
- *I drink wine, beer, or hard liquor*
- *I eat too much or snack between meals*
- *I blame others when things go wrong*
- *I am slow to admit I am wrong and argue a lot*
- *I drive over the speed limit*
- *I bite my nails*
- *My temper flares up whenever things don't go right*
- *I make sarcastic and cutting remarks*
- *I buy things impulsively, without thinking it through*
- *I waste too much time day-dreaming*
- *I have trouble getting up in the morning*
- *I avoid new people and new situations*
- *I read unhealthy and worthless books and magazines*
- *I talk too much about the opposite sex*
- *I am noisy and obnoxious*
- *I clown around whenever serious topics are discussed*
- *I talk too much about myself*
- *It is easy for me to lie my way out of a tough situation*
- *I boast and exaggerate to make myself look better*
- *I enjoy repeating negative information which I've hear about others*
- *I waste too much time watching TV*
- *I worry about things over which I have little control*
- *I spend too much time in front of the mirror*

IF BAD HABITS START AND ARE DICTATED BY THE MIND, IT STANDS TO REASON THAT NEW, HEALTHY HABITS WOULD ALSO BE CONTROLLED BY OUR THINKING.

God knows that the mind is very important in dictating what good things we will do. That is why He said in:

Ephesians 4:22-23 (Living Bible)
22) "then throw off your old evil nature--the old you that was a partner in your evil ways--rotten through and through, full of lust and sham.
23) "Now your attitudes and thoughts must all be constantly changing for the better."

The question remains, however, as to how we get our mind thinking right so that we will act better. God gives us the answer to this in:

2 Corinthians 10:5
"We are destroying speculations and every lofty thing raised up against the knowledge of God, and we are taking every thought captive to the obedience of Christ."

* *According to II Cor. 10:5 what does God want us to do with all of our thoughts?* ______________________________

____

AN IMPORTANT PROJECT FOR CLEANSING OUR MINDS

LET'S SUPPOSE YOU HAVE A BAD HABIT OF MAKING SARCASTIC AND CUTTING REMARKS TO OTHERS

You don't want that bad habit anymore, but want to form a new healthy habit of saying kind things to others. After you have prayed about the problem and your desire for a new habit you are now ready to begin.

A. Memorize one or two verses that explain WHY God does not want you to make cutting and sarcastic remarks.

You may want to memorize:

Ephesians 4:29-30
29) "Let no unwholesome word proceed from your mouth, but only such a word as is good for edification according to the need of the moment, that it may give grace to those who hear.
30) "And do not grieve the Holy Spirit of God, by whom you were sealed for the day of redemption."

As you go to sleep at night, concentrate on the above verse and think deeply why God does not want you to make cutting and sarcastic remarks. While driving to school and walking down the halls going to classes, have your mind dwell on these powerful thoughts from God. This exercise will be difficult at first because your mind is not accustomed to doing this.

B. After You Have Completed This First Exercise of Memorizing Verses That Talk About How God Is Against the Bad Habit

Memorize a verse or two about how God wants you to say only loving and kind things. For example:

Proverbs 16:23-24
23) "The heart of the wise teaches his mouth, and adds persuasiveness to his lips.
24) "Pleasant words are a honeycomb, sweet to the soul and healing to the bones."

As you go to sleep at night, concentrate on the above verse and think deeply on how beautiful and gracious these words are and how much they please God.

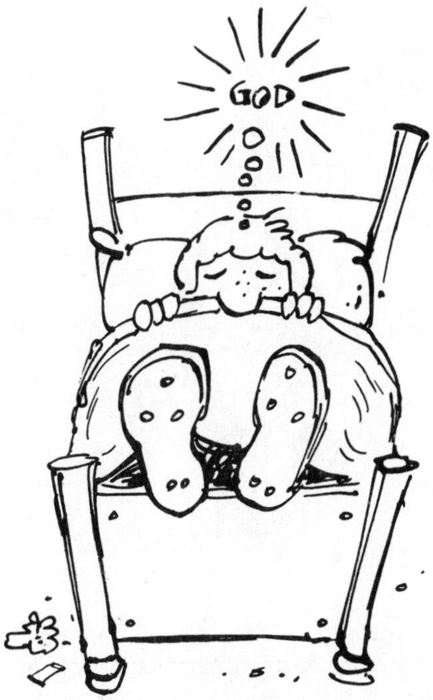

While driving to school, and walking down the halls going to class, have your mind dwell on the positive, powerful thoughts from God through His Word.

C. Pray Through What You Have Memorized

You have now memorized and are concentrating on both the negative and positive verses on God's kind of speech; the next thing to do is to repeat in prayer to God what you have memorized from His Word.

Model Prayer of Praying Through Scripture

"Dear God, I want to be a wise person. I know, Lord, that a wise person uses careful and persuasive speech. God, you say in your Word that sarcastic and cutting words are not pleasing to you, but gracious words are like honey--enjoyable and healthful. So Lord, thank you that I can form a new habit of saying gracious and loving statements to others."

D. THEN SPEND TIME PRAISING GOD FOR HOW HE'S HELPING YOU WITH YOUR TONGUE.

Praising God is a beautiful and life changing experience. As you praise God for what He is doing in your life, He will fill you with new joy and power.

You might want to praise God for who He is; for His work in your life; for His Word; ....Think about what you could say:

GOD I PRAISE YOU FOR . . .

____

____

____

____

____

____

____

____

____

Each night you could go to sleep by thinking through the negative and positive verses about gracious words. After meditating on these verses, you could pray them back to God and then spend time praising Him for who He is and what He is doing in your life through this new habit. Try this exercise at night, in the morning, to and from school, and at work. <u>You will soon begin to see the formation of a good new habit in your life</u>. God will be working through Scripture, prayer, and praise to renew your mind and give you a whole new pattern of living.

IMPORTANT SPECIAL NOTE

There are verses in the Bible on just about any new, healthy habit you may want to form. Usually, you can find a negative verse on the bad habit as well as positive verses on the new, healthy habit. Ask your youth worker or pastor to help you find these verses or get a Bible concordance and find them for yourself. As you memorize, meditate, pray and praise God, He will replace bad habits with new healthy ones.

III. If We are Going to Form New, Healthy Habits, We Need to Plan How We are Actually Going to Do It.

No new, healthy habit can form in our lives unless we finally get down to actually doing a good deed over and over again. God teaches us that right actions lead to right living. He speaks of this in:

Colossians 3:12-13
12) "And so, as those who have been chosen of God, holy and beloved, put on a heart of compassion, kindness, humility, gentleness and patience;
13) "bearing with one another, and forgiving each other, whoever has a complaint against any one; just as the Lord forgave you, so also should you."

✱ ***According** to the above passage, what are some positive actions that God wants His children to perform?* ______________________________

____

____

HOW DO WE BEGIN AN ACTION THAT WILL LEAD TO A GOOD HEALTHY HABIT?

LET'S ASSUME FOR A MOMENT...

that we would like to form the habit of having a quiet time with God. We have decided to get up and spend about a half hour in prayer and Bible study at 7 a.m.

1. PRAY ABOUT THIS NEW ACTION OF HAVING A QUIET TIME

The night before as you get ready to go to sleep, go over the positive and negative verses of meeting with God. (Your negative verses may need to deal with laziness.) Pray and thank God for the Holy Spirit and that you will have the desire and the power to actually get up and do what you know He wants you to do.

2. RESIST YOUR SIN NATURE THAT DOESN'T WANT YOU TO GET UP

Be wise about your schedule of priorities--go to bed early if you plan to get up early. As the alarm goes off at 6:50 a.m., you may very well have a battle on your hands. Your tired (but mostly lazy) body will want to continue sleeping. Your sin nature will tell you that it's not worth it to get up in the morning to meet with God. You will want to rationalize that you couldn't concentrate anyway. Resist all of this rationalization. Tell your sin nature that in the power of Christ, you don't have to listen to its reasoning. Claim the power of the Holy Spirit as you arise from your bed.

3. NOW JUST SIT DOWN AND DO IT

You may not feel like having a quiet time as you first start your new habit. Satan and your old sin nature will fight you as you try. But, God's Spirit is in you and as you obey God, He will give you a joy and desire--do not trust what your old nature is feeling. Let your will tell your emotions what you are going to do. Remember, it takes 21 days before a person is comfortable with a new action and approximately another 21 days before a new habit is formed. So hang in there and do what you know you should do no matter how you feel.

4. NOW THANK GOD THAT IN HIS POWER YOU DID IT!

Just as you are finishing your time with God stop and praise Him for who He is and what He is doing in your life. Thank Him for working in you and lifting you up into His presence. Thank Him that He is working in you to form new, healthy habits for His name's sake. As you praise and thank Him for what He has done, He will put in you a desire to praise and thank Him again.

5. RECOMMIT TO HAVING A QUIET TIME AGAIN THE NEXT DAY

As you finish your quiet time, rededicate yourself to meet Him again the next day for your special time together. Tell Him that you once again need Him to do His will through you. Anticipate what a meaningful time you are going to have the next day as you meet together.

In order to start a new activity that will lead to a healthy habit, we must have a plan that we can follow that will assure us of success.

IV. GOD WANTS US TO KEEP TRYING EVEN IF WE FAIL AT OUR FIRST FEW ATTEMPTS OF FORMING NEW HEALTHY HABITS.

Many people start out with intentions of forming new habits but after a failure or two they give up and go back to their own ways.

What these people fail to understand is that they are locked in a major spiritual war and the battle to form new habits is not an easy one.

A. God Hasn't Given Up on Us

God wants us to persevere in our fight for a new living style. God is more concerned than we that we develop good habits. He has the ability to see the potential within us, and that potential is developed as we let Him live His life through us. Since God is all patient, He does not easily give up on us, but is steadily working and waiting for us to be successful in a meaningful Christian life-style.

We need to persevere. The Bible says:

2 Timothy 2:13
"If we are faithless, He remains faithful; for He cannot deny Himself."

B. God Knows Us, He Knows Our Weaknesses

God does know our weaknesses and is not taken by surprise when we fail. But since He doesn't give up on us when we fail, He doesn't expect us to give up on ourselves or His power either. He talked about this in:

Hebrews 12:12-13
12) "Therefore, strengthen the hands that are weak and the knees that are feeble,
13) "and make straight paths for your feet, so that the limb which is lame may not be put out of joint, but rather be healed."

C. There's No Problem That You and God Can't Beat

God wants us to know that our striving against our old sin nature is tough. But, at the same time, He promises us that there will always be an escape if we trust Him with it. He says in:

1 Corinthians 10:13
"No temptation has overtaken you but such as is common to man; and God is faithful, who will not allow you to be tempted beyond what you are able, but with the temptation will provide the way of escape also, that you may be able to endure it."

It pleases the Lord very much when we decide that we are going to stick with Him even if we fail from time to time. It pleases the Lord that we decide to stick until we get the victory of forming habits that will set us free.

We can know that God can turn our failure into success and make our lives beautiful no matter how many times we have failed in the past.

IN CONCLUSION ...

There isn't anything quite like being filled with God's Spirit and walking free from the bondage of an unhealthy life style. The Christian life is a constant adventure where we by faith put off the wrong practices of our sin nature and put on the godly actions which come from Jesus Christ. As we fight and put on this new life style in Jesus, we can be assured that the battle is well worth every ounce of energy we spend. That is why God says:

1 Corinthians 15:58
"Therefore, my beloved brethren, be steadfast, immovable, always abounding in the work of the Lord, knowing that your toil is not in vain in the Lord."

NOTES

How to live in a

BROKEN HOME

One of the most important areas of our life is our relationships with our parents. A number of people affect our lives -- friends, teachers, employers, brothers and sisters -- but none have quite the effect on us as our parents do. For many of us, the relationships we have with our parents are, for the most part, pretty good. Sure we have some disagreements, hurt feelings, and misunderstandings, but usually our family operates in a spirit of harmony and love.

Maybe you are not as fortunate. You may live in a home where there is little or no love and harmony. You find yourself lying awake at night listening to your parents fight, wondering if all the bitterness will ever end and perhaps being afraid it might end. You fight the insecurity of being caught in the middle of your parents' distrust and hatred for one another. You are one of those who live in a fractured home--these types of experiences can be a nightmare.

PROJECT

WHAT IT'S LIKE

✱ *If you are from a broken home, list some of the difficulties and frustrations you face because of it.*

✱ *If you are not from a broken home, try to imagine and list what you think must be some of the frustrations of those living in a broken home.*

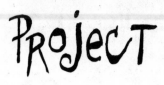

Our relationship with our family is so important, it can affect the way we think and act the rest of our lives. Being involved in a split family can be extremely traumatic and affects us in a dramatic way in the future. Because this is true, it is absolutely essential that we respond to the difficult situation of living in a broken home God's way.

LET'S DISCUSS TOGETHER SOME BASIC COUNSEL FROM SCRIPTURE, WHICH IF APPLIED WILL HELP YOU COPE WITH THE PROBLEMS OF LIVING IN A BROKEN HOME.

THE BIBLE COUNSELS US THAT GOD IS CLOSELY INVOLVED IN YOUR DIFFICULT SITUATION

A. GOD WILL BE CLOSE TO YOU

It is not God's will that your parents have deep conflicts, and He is grieved that the whole situation is taking place. He hates arguments, cruelties, insecurities, and the resulting tears. But God has given you and your parents a free will. Each member of your family has to decide whether or not he or she will live life in obedience to God. When any member of your family chooses not to exhibit or live God's love in your home, damage is going to be done and people within and outside of your family are going to be hurt.

AN INNOCENT BYSTANDER

You may be an innocent bystander who is suffering from the disobedience to God of some other member in your family. God is totally aware of what has happened and what you are feeling. He also knows how important it is that you have a good father/mother model and relationship so that you may develop as a well-rounded person.

GOD STEPS IN

When God sees that due to someone else's disobedience, you do not have that good relationship with your parents, God Himself steps in and provides the love, security, and direction that a mother and a father are designed to give. In a supernatural way, God, in a special way during this traumatic and trying time in your life, wants His presence experienced by you as never before.

King David, who understood rejection, contemplated being rejected by his parents. As he thought of these things happening, God shared with him a tremendous truth.

Psalm 27:10 (Living Bible)
"For if my father and mother should abandon me, you would welcome and comfort me."

✳ *Can you think of some way that God would like to welcome and comfort you in your difficulties of living in a broken home?*

____

____

____

The bigger the heartbreak you may have over your home situation, the more sufficient God is for you and He will make Himself real to you. The Bible says in:

Psalm 34:18
"God is near to the broken hearted, and saves those who are crushed in spirit."

B. GOD IS SOMEONE ON WHOM YOU CAN DEPEND

God will show you as He draws closer to you that He is a dependable God -- one who is always stable. Let's face it, friends may come and go, the security of a home can be ripped from us, our jobs may be gone in a moment's notice, but God remains the only true predictable one.

The Psalmist explained just how secure we are in God in:

Psalm 46:1-2
1) "God is our refuge and strength, a very present help in trouble.
2) "Therefore we will not fear, though earth should change, and though the mountains slip into the heart of the sea."

This passage can easily be paraphrased to explain what God is like when we face a difficulty with parents that are fighting.

A LOOSE PARAPHRASE OF PSALM 46 APPLYING TO YOUR HOME

> *"God is a person who will give us His security when the security of our parents' understanding is not there. He will not only give us His security, but also His strength to help us when we are weak. God is immediately with us when our parents fight or go through divorce proceedings. Therefore, we are not going to let fear and anxiety grip us even if our parents blame us for their hatred or we are caught in the middle of a family quarrel."*

God is the only one we can count on to never let us down. Though the Scripture teaches us we are to respect our parents, we must not expect them to be free of faults. We open ourselves up for a big letdown if we put our mother and father on a high pedestal. But Jesus can be put on a pedestal for He is trustworthy.

He said in Hebrews 13:5
"I will never desert you, nor will I ever forsake you."

C. God, a Strong God

God has the love and sensitivity to draw close to us when we are confused, hurt, and insecure due to family quarreling. We can, in turn, put our trust in Him because He is dependable at all times. We can also know that God is strong enough to pull us through this rugged situation.

God knew long before you were ever born that you would be going through the broken home crisis. God is also aware just how weak emotionally you and I really are. The Psalmist spoke of this in:

Psalm 103:14
"For He Himself knows our frame, He is mindful that we are but dust."

That's why God in no way wants you to face this difficult time in your life all by yourself. He wants to put His strength right inside you so that with His power you can be triumphant.

He says in:

Isaiah 41:10
"'Do not fear, for I am with you; do not anxiously look about you, for I am your God. I will strengthen you, surely I will help you, surely I will uphold you with My righteous right hand.'"

* According to the above passage, God tells us that there are two reactions we shouldn't have when a crisis comes along. What are they? ______________________________

____

* Why shouldn't we have those reactions? ______________________________

____

* What does God promise to do for us in times of great stress? ___

____

____

IMPORTANT! It's up to You.

God wants you to experience His nearness, stability, and strength at this trying time in your life. He wants you to know just how real He is and how great He can be. <u>But in order to experience His greatness in your life, you must by an act of the will believe what He has promised you in the Bible about your situation</u>. If you will believe these promises by faith, God will move to make this disastrous time become one of the most meaningful times of your life.

You will be able to say:

Psalm 34:8 (Living Bible)
"Oh, put God to the test and see how kind He is! See for yourself the way His mercies shower down on all who trust in Him."

II. The Bible Counsels You Who Live in a Broken Home To Be His Special Kind of Peacemaker

If you come from a broken home you are not living in an easy situation. There may be a major war taking place right in front of your eyes.

Both parents may be coming to you separately telling their side of the story, each trying to win your allegiance against the other. You may even be accused of being the one who is causing the problems. Your parents may be fighting one another and taking out their frustrations on you.

BECAUSE ALL OF THIS IS HAPPENING, YOU ARE CALLED UPON TO BE GOD'S SPECIAL KIND OF PEACEMAKER.

What is God's Special Kind of Peacemaker?

God's special kind of peacemaker is a person who can bring hurt, angry, or disagreeing people together in harmony through an example of love, gentleness, and understanding.

Jesus Himself is called "The Prince of Peace." God wants all Christians, whether or not from a broken home, to be conformed to the likeness of Christ. Living in a broken home gives you a unique chance to learn to be a peacemaker in the likeness of Christ. This tough but helpful training through living in a broken home can help you learn the secret of being God's special kind of peacemaker.

A. God's Special Kind of Peacemaker Must Be a Servant.

This learning to be a servant towards your fighting parents is not easy. We tend to think that somehow they should be serving us as we mature and are learning to be on our own. Then suddenly we find that they need all kinds of help from us, the kind of assistance we think they should be giving us. We need understanding from them but even more they seem to need understanding from us.

Attitudes and Actions of Servanthood

Here is a small list of attitudes and actions you might have thought you were entitled to receive from your parents. But you found that you must instead give those very same attitudes and actions back to them:

- *A spirit of understanding*
- *Time*
- *A sense of stability*
- *A willingness to listen*
- *A spirit of patience*
- *A willingness to forgive*
- *A willingness to exercise self-control*
- *A willingness to provide for the family*

It is a shock to find out that we must be servants to our parents and learn to give at such a young age. This giving on our part is difficult because our old nature is so selfish and self-centered. At first we might think that when Jesus the "King of Kings" came to earth, He would expect service toward Himself, but this was not the case. God talks about this attitude of Jesus in Matthew 20:28.

Matthew 20:28
"just as the Son of Man did not come to be served, but to serve, and to give His life a ransom for many."

Consequently, if we want to be God's special kind of peacemaker, and be like Christ we too must be willing to give in an unselfish way to our parents.

PROJECT

ATTITUDES AND ACTIONS OF SERVANTHOOD

List some practical ways you can be a servant right now where you are to your fighting parents:

It is difficult to give and give to our parents, especially when there seems to be such little response on their part. However, God wants to teach us to give to others even when there is little or no action on their part.

That's why the Bible says in:

Philippians 2:3
"Do nothing from selfishness or empty conceit, but with humility of mind let each of you regard one another as more important than himself."

B. God's Special Kind of Peacemaker Must Learn Not to Take Sides or Try to Punish Their Parents

It is not easy to avoid taking sides when your parents fight. In many cases, your parents may encourage you to get involved on their particular side of the dispute. It also seems easy to pick out who is at fault and who isn't when two sides have conflicts. But when you begin to really investigate you will find that there are two sides to the problem. If you listen to the whole story from both sides about the conflict, you will find that both sides are convincing. That is why the Bible says in:

Proverbs 18:17 (Living Bible)
"Any story sounds true until someone tells the other side and sets the record straight."

You really can't get all the facts about your parents' disagreement so as to pass judgment and take sides. Only God is able to get all the facts and weigh all the motives of your parents. It is God's job to pass judgment and take sides--it is not your job or responsibility.

Proverbs 16:2
"All the ways of a man are clean in his own sight, but the Lord weighs the motives."

Here is some information about your parents and their motives that would be hard or impossible to find out.

- *Bad attitudes or actions that took place before you were born.*
- *Their own parents' treatment of them.*
- *What their sex life is like.*
- *What mom thinks about herself as a homemaker.*
- *What it's like for dad at work and how that affects him.*
- *Things that were said between your mom and dad when you weren't there.*
- *What mom and dad really think about their financial situation.*
- *What has happened to them spiritually and why.*

Even if you could get all the information <u>you are not the one</u> to step into the disruption anyway. Your parents for the most part still see you as "their little child" and you do not carry the authority to step in. If you try to get involved directly to straighten them out you will just be torn apart emotionally. God does not want that to take place.

Proverbs 26:17 (Living Bible)
"Yanking a dog's ears is no more foolish than interfering in an argument that isn't any of your business."

YOUR INFLUENCE WITH YOUR PARENTS IS TO BE ONE OF AN EXAMPLE OF LOVE AND UNDERSTANDING NOT ONE OF JUDGE.

God never has given us the responsibility of taking revenge on our parents for what they have done to us or to one another. To take on that responsibility will only make matters worse, for both us and them. If there is any punishing to be done, God is the one who will do it--not us.

He says in:

Romans 12:19-21
19) "Never take your own revenge, beloved, but leave room for the wrath of God, for it is written, 'Vengeance is Mine, I will repay,' says the Lord.
20) "But if your enemy is hungry, feed him, and if he is thirsty, give him a drink; for in so doing you will heap burning coals upon his head.
21) "Do not be overcome by evil, but overcome evil with good."

God has ways of avenging those who do wrong to others. He knows when, where and how to punish those who do wrong. It's easy to think that one or both of our parents is being cruel to the other or us and is getting away with it. In reality, this is not the case. If either one or both of your parents are wronging you or others, they are already paying a price.

WHAT ARE SOME WAYS GOD MAY BE ALLOWING ONE OR BOTH OF YOUR FIGHTING PARENTS TO PAY FOR THE WRONG THEY ARE DOING?

- *Not experiencing the joy of the Lord*
- *Bitterness*
- *Frustration*
- *Unhappy relationships with others who are around them*
- *Financial problems*

Even if one or both of your parents was totally cruel to you or one another and never suffered on this earth for it, they still must face God who will ultimately judge all men according to their deeds. God speaks of this in:

2 Corinthians 5:10 (Living Bible)
"For we must all stand before Christ to be judged and have our lives laid bare--before him. Each of us will receive whatever he deserves for the good or bad things he has done in his earthly body."

It is easy to see why God does not want you to take sides between your parents or try to avenge what they may have done to one another. You can rest with perfect ease that God will handle the difficult situation in His time and in His way. What your parents need from you is love and compassion.

C. God's Special Kind of Peacemaker Must Learn to Be a Healer by What is Said.

What we say is such a powerful force in life. By our words, we can express love or hate, kindness or cruelty, praise or cursing. God wants you to communicate to **your** *parents in this difficult time in the way that would be most pleasing to Him and help heal the pain in your home.*

OUR WORDS ARE MOST HEALING WHEN WE ARE NOT SCREAMING OR HARSH.

It is easy to become so frustrated in our homes that we lash out or yell at those who are hurting us. It's even easier to be yelling when our parents are screaming at us. But often the action that is the easiest to do will cause the greatest amount of damage if it is done.

God does not want you raising your voice or being harsh with your parents. God knows that when you do it, no matter what the circumstances, it is a mistake.

GOD EXPLAINS IN SCRIPTURE WHAT A SOFT OR HARSH ANSWER WILL DO

Proverbs 15:1
"A gentle answer turns away wrath, but a harsh word stirs up anger."

* *Can you think of some reason why a soft answer can help keep your parents calm?* ______________________________

* *Can you think of some reasons why harsh words cause a quarrel?* __

OUR WORDS ARE MOST HEALING WHEN WE SPEAK THE TRUTH IN A KIND AND LOVING WAY.

God does not expect us to suppress our feelings, thoughts, and words from our parents. He wants us to "clear the air" about the way we feel. If you share what you are feeling you may help your parents understand how serious their fighting is.

But God does not want us to simply blast the truth at our parents without kindness. God gives us the guidelines about our conversation towards our parents in:

Proverbs 3:3-5 (Living Bible)
3) "Never forget to be truthful and kind. Hold these virtues tightly. Write them deep within your heart.
4,5) "If you want favor with both God and man, and a reputation for good judgment and common sense, then trust the Lord completely; don't ever trust yourself."

* According to the passage (Prov. 3:3-5), what two virtues should we have? ______________________________

____

* How important should these virtues be to us? ______________

____

* What will be the results if we practice these virtues? ______

____

We must be truthful with our parents, but we in no way should be cutting or cruel as we speak the truth.

Proverbs 12:18
"There is one who speaks rashly like the thrusts of a sword, but the tongue of the wise brings healing."

Right Responses and Wrong Responses in What We Say

For example...

Let's talk about an example situation where your father is verbally cutting down your mother and telling you just how awful he thinks she is.

THE WRONG WAY OF RESPONDING WOULD BE TO SAY:

"I can't stand the way you are always cutting mother down. I'm sick of it. Why don't you grow up and think of something good to say about her for a change."

THE RIGHT WAY OF RESPONDING WOULD BE TO SAY:

"Dad, I realize mom has some faults, but it's hard for me emotionally when you say cruel things about her. I am trying to think of reasons why I should love her more. I would really appreciate it if you could help me with this."

Another example...

Let's assume for a moment that your mom asks you to lie to your dad if he should ask you whether your mom is dating some other man.

THE WRONG RESPONSE:

"Look, mom, Jesus Christ is king of my life and I have no intentions of lying. If you don't have a clear conscience about dating this guy, then you shouldn't be doing it. When are you going to get your life together?"

THE RIGHT RESPONSE:

"Mother, you know how much I love you and want to please you. But on moral issues such as this, I cannot go against what God says to do and God commands me not to lie. I love you but if dad asks me about this, I plan on telling him the truth.

PROJECT

RIGHT WORDS RESPONSE

Think of four other instances where you might be called upon to answer your parents in truth kindness.

Think of a wrong response. Then write out the right response with kind wording.

III. The Third Part of God's Counsel Is to Be Joyful and Thankful That God Has Us Right Where He Wants Us.

God hates sin and the awful affect it has on others. Yet God can use even the awful things that happen to us to do great things in our lives. God is not taken by surprise that we may be in a broken home; He knows it and wants to use it to help make something beautiful in our lives. Sure it is hard and ugly to live in a broken home, but that is no reason for us to feel sorry for ourselves. God gives us several reasons why we can still be thankful and rejoice in the middle of a tragedy in our lives. If we respond positively to living in a broken home, that is if we respond God's way, He will teach us:

A. We Will Learn How to Obey God Even More

Suffering teaches us that God is the only person who is worth following and obeying. When we are going through a crisis (such as living in a broken home), we realize that a lot of other things in life are secondary in comparison to the peace of mind that only God can give. We learn that obeying God is a positive way to get peace of heart. Jesus Christ knew this truth as He lived an example of total faith in God.

B. Living in a Broken Home Teaches Us to Be Thankful.

When we live in a broken home, we soon learn that God is the only certainty we have. Anything given to us beyond that is strictly a gift; a gift for which we should be thankful. When we live in a broken home and have our security ripped from us we can then learn how to be thankful for little everyday things.

Here is a list of things for which a person from a broken home can be thankful:

- *Friends*
- *Education*
- *Food*
- *Clothes*
- *The Bible*
- *Transportation*
- *A place to live*
- *The beauty of nature*
- *Our health*

Actually, if we are from a broken home and we are willing, we can become a joyful and a thankful people. Because we have faced some difficulty, we can learn to say with Paul:

Philippians 4:11-13
11) "Not that I speak from want; for I have learned to be content in whatever circumstances I am.
12) "I know how to get along with humble means, and I also know how to live in prosperity; in any and every circumstance I have learned the secret of being filled and going hungry, both of having abundance and suffering need.
13) "I can do all things through Him who strengthens me."

C. Living in a Broken Home Teaches Us How to Forgive.

Living in a broken home is a traumatic experience that will affect our lives forever. This effect can be fantastic depending on the response of the person involved. Unless a person from a broken home learns in the power of Christ how to forgive those who have hurt him, he or she will not be able to experience God's happiness the rest of their lives. But on the other hand, if a person can forgive, he is on his way to being a person who loves. There is nothing better than for us to learn how to love. Since life is full of injustices, we are constantly faced with the decision as to whether we will forgive others or choose to be unforgiving. A person who can forgive and be a real peacemaker discovers the joy of real loving. Those of us in a broken home can learn this vital lesson early in life. We actually practice what God asks us to do in:

Colossians 3:13
"Bearing with one another, and forgiving each other, whoever has a complaint against any one; just as the Lord forgave you, so also should you."

D. God Can Teach Us Some Truths Through Suffering in a Broken Home That We Can Use to Help Others in This Same Predicament.

Sad to say, but if you live in a broken home, you have much in common with a growing number of people. More and more students are becoming the victims of a fractured home life. Because this is true, you could be given the chance to help many students who are going through just what you are facing. You can actually comfort them in some of the same ways that God has comforted you. If you respond the right way to a broken home, God can greatly use you in the years to come in the lives of others.

God speaks of your doing this:

2 Corinthians 1:3-5
3) "Blessed by the God and Father of our Lord Jesus Christ, the Father of mercies and God of all comfort;
4) "who comforts us in all our affliction so that we may be able to comfort those who are in any affliction with the comfort with which we ourselves are comforted by God.
5) "For just as the sufferings of Christ are ours in abundance, so also our comfort is abundant through Christ."

IN CONCLUSION . . .

If you live in a broken home you are going through one of the most emotionally traumatic crises of your life. How you deal with this crisis will greatly affect you; in fact, it will set the pattern for the rest of your life. God has told us how He wants us to respond to life's difficult situations. If you obey His plan in this matter, you will have a life of joy and peace.

It's true that you will be living at home only a few more years, but how you handle your home situation is of vital importance. It is crucial that we leave home with an obedient attitude toward God and a good attitude about life.

Would you be willing to commit yourself in God's power to be His special kind of peacemaker in your fighting home?

How to deal with GUILT

We live in an age where open rebellion against God and His ways runs rampant. Outside of the power of God in the Christian's life there is little restraint around us to deter us from thinking thoughts and doing acts that go against God's holiness and our own conscience. Not only does the Christian live in a nation full of sin, but the true believer soon discovers that he/she has his old sin nature with which to contend. The Bible teaches us that there is a great spiritual battle taking place in which Satan and his demonic helpers are out to do all they can to destroy the Christian.

Yet, countless Christians find themselves thinking thoughts and living lives that are displeasing to God and a source of true guilt in themselves. The feeling that God does not really love us and guilt from sin are two of the biggest problems facing American students.

God never intended Christians to be miserable. He hates sin and its consequences--guilt and death. God reveals in Scripture what we are to do when sin and guilt invade our lives.

KING DAVID -

A MAN WHO WAS WEIGHED DOWN WITH TRUE GUILT

In the Old Testament, we find a man, King David, who walked after God seeking to please the Lord in all that he did. But one day he got himself into all kinds of trouble. While walking on the roof of his house one evening, David saw a beautiful woman, Bathsheba, taking a bath. David decided that even though she was married to someone else, he would have sexual relations with her. He figured that he would have his kicks and that would be that. But it wasn't long until Bathsheba reported back to him that she was pregnant. The problem that David now faced was even more complicated since Bathsheba's hubsand, Uriah was off to war and it would be obvious that Uriah could not have gotten her pregnant. Instead of dealing with his sin problem immediately, David proceeded to fall deeper into the awfulness of rebellion by trying to cover up his sin. The King became so desperate that he arranged for Uriah to be killed on the battlefield. By this time David was deep in guilt, but he refused to go before God to get things right. Instead God came to David through the prophet Nathan and revealed His great displeasure to David for the sin he had committed.

For the entire story of David and Bathsheba, see 2 Samuel 11:1 through 2 Samuel 12:28.

When God spoke with David, he was plunged into even deeper guilt. He knew that he must once again get back into fellowship with a loving but holy God.

PSALM 51 AN IMPORTANT CHAPTER ABOUT GUILT

In Psalm 51 God reveals the stirring account of the prayer that King David prayed to have his guilt removed and his fellowship with God restored. The principles found in Psalm 51 tell us much about

- *the character of God*
- *true repentance*
- *God's dealing with a guilt ridden person*
- *how God can restore a guilt-scarred person*

Since God does not change, the principles revealed in Psalm 51 can be applied to our lives when we also find ourselves in the anguish of sin and guilt.

I. The First Principle Learned from Psalm 51 Is That a Guilt-Ridden Christian's Only Hope for Forgiveness Lies in the Character of God.

King David began his plea to God by praying.

Psalm 51:1
"Be gracious to me, O God, according to Thy lovingkindness; according to the greatness of Thy compassion blot out my transgressions."
David realized that his only hope for forgiveness lay in the infinite love of God. Only God's amazing character--which shows itself in many forms of love--counts when a person comes to Him for cleansing.
When we fall into sin, our hope for forgiveness is not in something we have done, are doing, or will do for God in the future. Our hope lies in the fact that God's love is an amazing force that will never leave us.

What We Should and Should Not Say to God When We Are Caught in Sin and Guilt

We should not say to God:

God, forgive me because I never did this sin before.

God, forgive me because I used to lead a Bible study.

God, forgive me because I'm now having a consistent Quiet Time.

God, if You forgive me, I'll witness everyday from now on.

We would be wise to say to God:

God, forgive me for Your name's sake.

God, forgive me; I know You are so patient.

God, forgive me because Christ paid for all my sins and I trust His work alone.

God, please forgive me because I know that it's part of Your nature to be forgiving.

A. David Pleaded for God's Graciousness

Psalm 51:1
"Be gracious to me, O God, according to Thy lovingkindness; according to the greatness of Thy compassion blot out my transgressions."

WHAT IS GOD'S GRACIOUSNESS?

> *God's graciousness is that special type of tenderness and affection that He pours out on us even though we in no way can earn or deserve it.*

If it were not for the graciousness of God, no one would be able to come before Him; all would be doomed to eternal judgment. It is only through the Lord, showering undeserved tenderness and affection upon us, that we can ever hope to walk with Him.

The Bible is very clear on the subject of our need for God's continued graciousness for our lives when it says in:

Psalm 130:3-4
3) "If Thou, Lord, shouldst mark iniquities, O Lord, who could stand?
4) "But there is forgiveness with Thee, that Thou mayest be feared."

✱ *According to the above verses, what do you think "who could stand" means?* ______________________________

✱ *If He did count our sins, do you think we could stand?* __________

____

✱ *Since God has forgiven us and not counted our sins against us, what response should we have?* ______________________________

____

IMPORTANT

God, however, does not simply ignore sin. Because of His holiness, God demands that every sin be counted and paid for. Since God is holy and we are not, we stand to pay for every sin we have ever committed. The penalty of our sin is death, total separation from God forever. But God, who is richer in love than any person can comprehend has given us the greatest undeserved gift possible--His Son Jesus Christ.

DAVID PLEADED FOR GOD'S LOVINGKINDNESS

He went on to say to God:

Psalm 51:1
"Be gracious to me, O God, according to Thy lovingkindness."

David saw that he was in great need of God's lovingkindness. We, too, as Christians must base our plea of forgiveness on God's great lovingkindness.

WHAT IS GOD'S LOVINGKINDNESS?

God's lovingkindness is His great love in action. It is God's infinite ability and desire to show us His love and goodness in a tangible way.

King David knew that God was a God who exercises lovingkindness. He said in another psalm:

Psalm 26:3
"For Thy lovingkindness is before my eyes, and I have walked in Thy truth."

God's love is not a passive affair. He demonstrates it in ways we can see and understand.

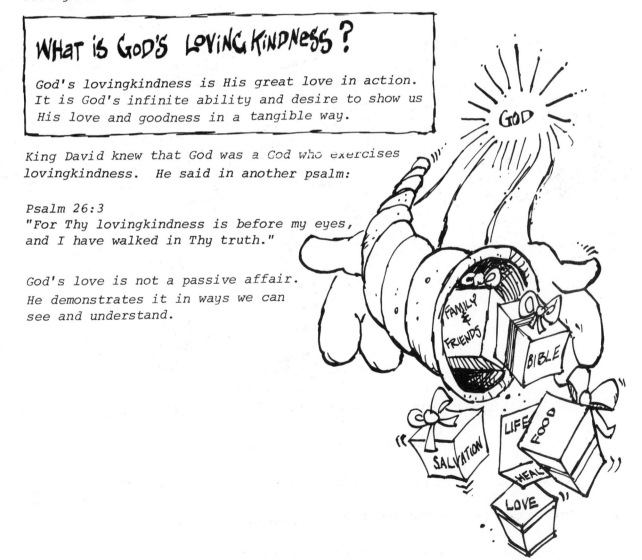

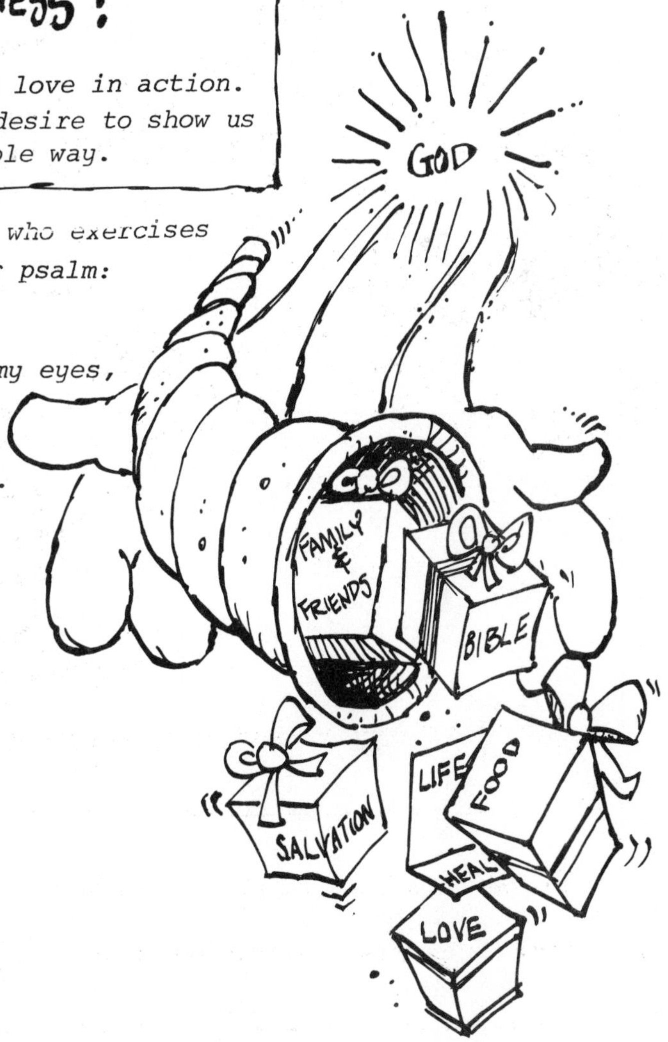

PROJECT

EXAMPLE OF GOD'S LOVINGKINDNESS

What are some ways that God shows us lovingkindness?

- *Became a man and walked among us*
- *Gives us food*

If there's ever a time when we need to see God's love in action towards us, it is when we have fallen deep into guilt. We need to see in a concrete way that God has not abandoned us or has lessened His love for us in any way.

Psalm 92:1-2
1) "It is good to give thanks to the Lord, and to sing praises to Thy name, O Most High;
2) "To declare Thy lovingkindness in the morning and Thy faithfulness by night."

We have seen that David built his hope for getting back into fellowship with God by trusting in God's character alone. He rested his entire case on the constant outpouring of God's love.

He trusted that God would blot out his sin because of the Lord's graciousness and lovingkindness. But David sensed that he was so deep in sin that he needed to plunge even further into God's love.

God wants us to see His love in action even when we are convinced that we don't deserve it. When God does show His lovingkindness, His hope is that we will respond to Him the right way--by loving and praising Him. God speaks of this in Psalm 92:1. "It is good to give thanks to the Lord, and to sing praises to Thy name, O Most High."

C. DAVID PLEADED FOR THE GREATNESS OF GOD'S COMPASSION

He said:

Psalm 51:1
"Be gracious to me, O God, according to Thy lovingkindness; according to the greatness of Thy compassion, blot out my transgressions."

WHAT IS GOD'S COMPASSION?

Compassion is God's everlasting desire and ability to exercise a deep and moving sense of pity towards those who are in great need.

While God hates our sin, he still loves us and is moved with pity towards us and our weaknesses. Being infinitely strong, God still sympathizes with all our weaknesses. That is why it says in:

Psalm 103:13-15 (Living Bible)
13) "He is like a father to us, tender and sympathetic to those who reverence him.
14) "For he knows we are but dust,
15) "and that our days are few and brief, like grass, like flowers,"

*Can you think of instances and areas in your life where your earthly father has had compassion for you? ______________________

____

According to Lamentations 3:22-23,

* *what do we know about God's compassion?* ______________________

____

____

*According to Psalm 103:13-15, what is it that God remembers about us? ____

____

David knew that even in the awfulness of his transgression, God would still have a deep moving compassion for him. God's willingness to sympathize and deal gently with us never wears out. There is a fantastic promise for us found in the Old Testament.

Lamentations 3:22-23
22) "The Lord's lovingkindnesses indeed never cease, for His compassions never fail.
23) "They are new every morning; great is Thy faithfulness."

THINK ABOUT IT

It is a natural desire for most people to want to bargain with God when they find themselves locked into sin and guilt. But God is not moved to cleanse our sin by the persuasiveness of our speech. Living in God's character is enough graciousness, lovingkindness, and compassion to absorb the ugliness of our sin and guilt. That is why, when we are drowned with guilt, we should throw ourselves at His feet and trust in His love shown at the cross.

How unbelievably fortunate we are to have a God who was described by the Prophet Micah:

Micah 7:18-19
18) "Who is a God like Thee, who pardons iniquity and passes over the rebellious act of the remnant of His possession? He does not retain His anger forever, because He delights in unchanging love.
19) "He will again have compassion on us; He will tread our iniquities underfoot. Yes, Thou wilt cast all their sins into the depths of the sea."

II. THE SECOND PRINICIPLE LEARNED FROM PSALM 51 IS WHAT TRUE REPENTANCE IS ALL ABOUT

A. REPENTANCE MEANS HAVING A BROKEN HEART OVER OUR SIN

David did not attempt to justify his actions or make excuses for himself. Instead, he came to God with an attitude of deep shame and humality.

Psalm 51:16-17
16) "For Thou dost not delight in sacrifice, otherwise I would give it; Thou art not pleased with burnt offering.
17) "The sacrifices of God are a broken spirit; a broken and a contrite heart, O God, Thou wilt not despise."

In David's day, the Jews would sacrifice certain animals to God by burning them on an altar. This was done in an attempt to find forgiveness for their sins and to satisfy God's justice.

* *According to Psalm 51:16, is there anything we can say or do for God that will cause Him to have compassion on us?* ____________

____

✱ According to Psalm 51:17, what type of an attitude is God looking for in us when we come to Him about our sin? ______________

____

WHAT IS A CONTRITE HEART?

A contrite heart says: "I realize that I have disobeyed a Holy God. His holiness, greatness, and authority leave me humble and submissive. I am guilty and deserve to be judged, but I humbly plead for His mercy.

David caught in the awfulness of his sin, was broken and contrite before the Lord. His repentant attitude is described further in:

Psalm 51:3
"For I know my transgressions, and my sin is ever before me."

THE AWFULNESS OF SIN!

David was overcome by the realization of his sin. The guilt of his wrongdoing was constantly upon his shoulders. He saw his sin for what it was--and it sickened him. Our sins ought to grieve us when we see the severe impact it has on our lives. When we see our sin as it is we ought to have a deep sense of sorrow and brokenness before God.

PROJECT

HOW DOES SIN DAMAGE OUR LIVES?

It shuts off our fellowship with God

It can turn into habits that rob us of our joy

It hurts God deeply

It can keep us from growing stronger in Christ

It can destroy our relationships with other people

It can leave us frustrated and defeated

It can ruin our witness for Christ

David realized the awful consequences of sin and it broke his heart. He looked at his life, saw the damage that had been done, and spoke again from a contrite heart.

"Behold, I was brought forth in iniquity, and in sin my mother conceived me."

David explains in the passage (Psalm 51:5) that not only had he sinned but that his very nature was sinful from the moment of his birth. He realized that he was a "sin-a-holic" and would always have a sinful nature within him. David did not use this as an excuse for his actions. He simply mentioned it as further evidence of his repentant heart.

B. Repentance Means Confession to God That We Have Sinned.

Confession of our Sin

Once David became aware of the awfulness of his sin and became broken and contrite before God, he took the next step of repentance--he humbly confessed his sin to God. We follow his words in:

Psalm 51:4
"Against Thee, Thee only, I have sinned, and done what is evil in Thy sight, so that Thou art justified when Thou dost speak and blameless when Thou dost judge."

King David knew that what he had done with Bathsheba and her husband, Uriah, could be explained in no other terms than that he had deliberately disobeyed God and His commands. He did not try to excuse his sin in any way. He just came before God with an attitude of brokenness and said, "I have sinned."

When we come to God to confess our sin, the first thing we should do is admit that we have disobeyed God and have sinned against God. He is not interested in our excuses, no matter how valid they seem. God is looking for us to agree with Him that we have in fact openly rebelled against Him.

God made a generous offer to the children of Israel after they had disobeyed Him. He told them what was expected of them in:

Jeremiah 3:12-13
12) "Go, and proclaim these words toward the north and say, 'Return, faithless Israel,' declares the Lord; 'I will not look upon you in anger, for I am gracious,' declares the Lord. 'I will not be angry forever.
13) "'Only acknowledge your iniquity, that you have transgressed against the Lord your God and have scattered your favors to the strangers under every green tree, and you have not obeyed My voice.' declares the Lord."

* According to Jer. 3:13, what is the one thing Israel had to do if it wanted to experience God's mercy? ____________________

____

David truly confessed his sin to God. He came before Him and agreed with God that he was a sinner through and through.

C. Repentance Means Turning from the Wrong We Have Done.

In his prayer to God, David showed his desire to forsake his sin by telling God over and over again this fact. The phrases are recorded in Psalm 51 and are as follows:

vs. 10 - Create in me a <u>clean</u> <u>heart</u>

vs. 10 - <u>Renew</u> a <u>steadfast</u> <u>spirit</u> within me

vs. 12 - Sustain me to a <u>willing</u> <u>spirit</u>

vs. 13 - I will teach transgressors Thy ways

vs. 14 - My tongue will joyfully sing of Thy righteousness

vs. 15 - My mouth may declare Thy praise

David knew that repentance involved turning away from sin and turning back to God. After seeing the awfulness of his sin, he had a new desire to leave his sin and follow after God.

We need to see our sin for what it is--

Deadly

Destroying

Disgusting

Heartbreaking

--to a holy God.

Only as we see sin for what it really is will we develop a repentant heart. A heart that says:

- *I have sinned against a holy God and deserve his judgment.*
- *I am thankful that Jesus paid for my sin and that, because of Him, I am no longer guilty before God.*
- *Because of God's great love and forgiveness towards me, I desire to forsake my sin and begin again to live a life that is pleasing to Him.*

The Bible sums up what repentance is when it says in:

Proverbs 28:13
"He who conceals his transgressions will not prosper, but he who confesses and forsakes them will find compassion."

III. ALSO, WE FIND IN PSALM 51 WHAT A GRACIOUS, LOVING, KIN AND COMPASSIONATE GOD WILL DO WITH THE SINS OF A REPENTANT MAN

A. GOD WILL BLOT OUT THE GUILTY PERSON'S TRANSGRESSIONS

David made a tremendous request to the Lord in:

Psalm 51:1
"Be gracious to me, O God, according to Thy lovingkindness; according to the greatness of Thy compassion blot out my transgressions."

David had an indictment of sin that was charged to his record before God. David had accumulated such a moral debt that no matter how much he tried, he could not pay back that debt to God. The indictment was so demanding and his debt so great that only eternal separation from God could be used to repay God. David did not want to die and live in total separation from God forever, so he asked that God would wipe his record clean.

God in no way could overlook David's great debt, and our debt is no different than David's. We too need to have the record against us wiped clean. God wiped David's slate completely clean so that he would never be charged for that sin again. This was not an easy thing for the Lord to do. He took David's indictment of sin and placed it all on Jesus Christ when He hung on the cross. We learn what happened to David's sin in:

Colossians 2:13,14 (Living Bible)
13) "You were dead in sins, and your sinful desires were not yet cut away. Then he gave you a share in the very life of Christ, for he forgave all your sins,
14) "and blotted out the charges proved against you, the list of his commandments which you had not obeyed. He took this list of sins and destroyed it by nailing it to Christ's cross."

According to verse 13 of Colossians 2, what has He done with all our sin? ________________________________

In Col. 2:14, God says that we all have a long list of debts that we cannot pay to God. Since we cannot pay this great certificate of debt, what has God done about it? __________

____

By applying what Christ was to do on the cross many years later, God was able to take David's indictment of sin and certificate of debt and simply erase what was on his terrible account. God has done the same thing with our rebellion stained record.

God wants us to know He is not sitting in heaven dwelling on our already forgiven/forgotten sins. He says in:

Isaiah 44:22
"I have wiped out your transgressions like a thick cloud, and your sins like a heavy mist. Return to Me, for I have redeemed you."

What do you think Isaiah 44:22 means? ________________

____

The only thing we can do is humble ourselves and praise God for His willingness to forgive us and put any remembrance of our past sin out of His mind forever. Since God is so in love with us and Christ has done such a great work at the cross, we can rejoice with the promise He gives us in:

Isaiah 43:25 (Living Bible)
"I, yes, I alone am he who blots away your sins for my own sake and will never think of them again."

B. GOD WILL ALSO WASH AND CLEANSE US FROM ALL OUR SIN

David, understanding God's way, asks the Lord to take Him even one step further in his search for removal of his guilt and renewed fellowship with the Lord. He asks the Lord to fully cleanse him of all his sin. Throughout David's intense prayer for forgiveness, he sought the Lord for cleansing. He said:

Psalm 51:2,7 (Living Bible)
2) "Oh, wash me, cleanse me from this guilt. Let me be pure again."
7) "Sprinkle me with the cleansing blood and I shall be clean again. Wash me and I shall be whiter than snow."

Sin and guilt are like deep penetrating pollution that soaks into every fiber of our soul. It is not as simple as having dirt on our hands that can easily be washed off. Rebellion toward God is a deep, embedded stain that takes a miraculous washing and cleansing that only God can do. God in His great love and power is able to reach down and completely purify layer after layer of our polluted lives and make us morally spotless. This is why God says in:

Isaiah 1:18
"'Come now, and let us reason together,' says the Lord, 'though your sins are as scarlet, they will be as white as snow; though they are red like crimson, they will be like wool.'"

* *What does it mean in Isaiah 1:18, "sins are as scarlet"?* ______________

____

GOD WILL TAKE THE EMBEDDED STAINS OF SIN AND MAKE THEM SPOTLESSLY WHITE

God has the greatest moral purifier in all the world in the blood of Christ that was shed at the cross. God speaks of this in:

Hebrews 10:22 (Living Bible)
"Let us go right in, to God Himself, with true hearts fully trusting Him to receive us, because we have been sprinkled with Christ's blood to make us clean, and because we have been washed with the pure water."

C. ONCE WE TRULY HAVE CONFESSED OUR SINS TO HIM, GOD WILL REFUSE TO LOOK AT OUR SINS ANY MORE.

King David asked a special request of the Lord in his repentant prayer.

Psalm 51:9
"Hide Thy face from my sins, and blot out all my iniquities."

David longed for God to smile at him once again. But how could God smile at David when the Lord had seen all that David had done?

God sees every wrong that we commit. Scripture points this fact out in:

Jeremiah 16:17
"For My eyes are on all their ways; they are not hidden from My face, nor is their iniquity concealed from My eyes."

GOD WILL REFUSE TO LOOK UPON OUR SINS

God looks at us through the moral purity of Jesus Christ who now lives in us. Instead of looking at our sin, God concentrates on what Christ did for us at the cross. God judged our sins at the cross and now He lovingly refuses to look at our sin anymore.

OFFER PRAISE TO GOD

There can only be praise offered to a God who so graciously wipes out our sin record, washes us to spotless purity, and refuses to look at our sin when we come to Him in repentance.

David understood what this attitude of praise is all about when he said:

Psalm 103:1-5
1) "Bless the Lord, O my soul; and all that is within me, bless His holy name.
2) "Bless the Lord, O my soul, and forget none of His benefits;
3) "Who pardons all your iniquities; who heals all your diseases;
4) "Who redeems your life from the pit; who crowns you with lovingkindness and compassion;
5) "Who satisfies your years with good things, so that your youth is renewed like the eagle."

IV. In Psalm 51 We Learn What a Gracious, Loving, Kind and Compassionate God Will Do for the Guilt-Ridden Person Who Repents of His Sins.

A person who has confessed his sin needs to realize that his life is not ruined. David realized this as he prayed that God would do a rebuilding work in his life.

A. God Will Give Back our Joy if We Confess our Sins Before Him.

David prayed that God would give back the joy that was once his in the Lord. He said in:

Psalm 51:8
"Make me to hear joy and gladness, let the bones which Thou hast broken rejoice."

In a powerful way God had crushed David because of his sin. God purposely put His hand on David to make Him miserable through guilt, fear, and worry so that he would come to his senses about his sins and repent. But God can heal as well as punish. He can, and will, replace every emotional pain brought on by guilt, with joy and gladness. The prophet Hosea put it well when he said:

Hosea 6:1 (Living Bible)
"Come, let us return to the Lord; it is He who has torn us - He will heal us. He has wounded - He will bind us up."

David needed assurance of his forgiveness from the Lord. He wanted to know and feel that all was well in his relationship with God. God was more than willing to oblige and help David in his need. In a supernatural way, God steps right into the emotions of a person and lets him know that all is well by flooding that person with real joy.

The best place for us to find renewed joy and gladness in the Lord is by reviewing God's Word and trusting His promises as revealed in the Bible. David learned this truth for he wrote:

Psalm 119:92-93 (Living Bible)
92) "I would have despaired and perished unless your laws had been my deepest delight.
93) "I will never lay aside your laws, for you have used them to restore my joy and health."

Any person who has confessed his sin has the right to expect the Lord to fill him with joy and gladness.

B. GOD WILL GIVE THE REPENTANT SINNER A NEW ATTITUDE

God will not only restore the repentant sinner with joy and gladness, but He will actually put a whole new attitude in the repentant person's heart.

King David continued to pray:

Psalm 51:10
"Create in me a clean heart, O God, and renew a steadfast spirit within me."

David, and all sinners, need not only to be saved, but also to be reformed as well. Because we are so wretched, we need a complete miracle in our lives for us to walk in a manner pleasing to God.

David knew that God is the only person who can create for the good. The King made a simple but beautiful request to the Lord. He asked God to create in him a clean heart. As a boy, young David had studied the detail and the magnificence of God's creation. David reasoned in his heart that a God who could create all of nature could surely create a clean heart in David. David, of course, was right about the Lord. God wants to create in us a whole new attitude about life and our response to Him.

There was a time in David's life when He was walking with the Lord. His attitude about God was right. But because of his outright rebellion and his deep guilt he had slipped away to a wrong attitude about God. During his time of sin, he had seen God as someone to ignore or escape. Then David's time of repentance came and he wanted God to bring him back to the right attitudes of worship and obedience.

David wanted the attitude he talked about in:

Psalm 57:7
"My heart is steadfast, O God, my heart is steadfast; I will sing, yes, I will sing praises!"

God is so powerful and loving that He can stir up and renew the right attitudes that we once had for Him. All the repentant sinner needs to do is ask God to renew the right attitudes in his life, believe God will do it, and it happens.

C. GOD WILL GIVE THE REPENTANT SINNER A MINISTRY FOR GOD'S WORK.

Many people feel that once they have greatly sinned against the Lord, and have deep guilt, they will never again be used by the Lord for a Christian ministry. But God teaches us in Psalm 51:12 that there is still much we can do for the Lord when we have repented of our sin. David prayed:

Psalm 51:12,13
12) "Restore to me the joy of Thy salvation, and sustain me with a willing spirit.
13) "Then I will teach transgressors Thy ways, and sinners will be converted to Thee."

Needless to say, God doesn't want us sinning and getting all hung up up in guilt. Sin always leaves its scars and does its damage on our lives. Yet God can rebuild a life so that one can serve Him again.

Realizing that God was forgiving Him, David wanted to be used by God again. He wanted to tell others of the wrong he had done so that they would not have to fall into the same trap. He wanted to lead others in the right way of living. God granted David's request. Although David still suffered greatly for his sin, we find that some of his greatest psalms were written after the affair with Bathsheba.

God can put any repentant sinner back into the ministry for Him. Only a God of love, power and compassion would be so gracious as to use us again after we have sinned.

It is no wonder that David wanted to once again praise the Lord with His life. He put it quite clear when he said in:

Psalm 51:14-15
14) "Deliver me from bloodguiltiness, O God, Thou God of my salvation; then my tongue will joyfully sing of Thy righteousness.
15) "O Lord, open my lips, that my mouth may declare Thy praise."

IN CONCLUSION

There is no God like the true and living God. He alone, with his Godly attributes, is big enough and gracious enough to forgive our sins and remove the guilt that goes with them. When we find ourselves in sin we need to trust in His loving character, repent from our sin and trust God to remove our sin and restore us to serving Him. If we do this, we will find that we can continue on living a life that is both pleasing to God and fulfilling to us.

NOTES

The Christian Student and

ROCK MUSIC

If there is one movement that characterizes our modern youth culture, it would be the sweeping appeal of secular "Rock Music."

For Example

More than 87% of America's youth clain that "Rock Music" is their favorite type of music.

According to a recent study the average high school student listens to 4 to 5 hours of "Rock Music" a day.

It is not uncommon to see a single rock album sell over three million copies.

Hundreds of thousands of students attend live rock concerts every year.

We live in an age where rock music and its performing personalities affect the way students think and live. We as Christians cannot escape a culture that is saturated by the powerful "rock" phenonema.

There is much confusion among many Christians about the effect and the wisdom of listening to or dwelling on rock music. The Bible does not address itself to rock music directly, but in Scripture we do find guidelines that can give us wisdom about how we as Christians should deal with "rock."

Since we as Christian students need to understand how to deal with rock, let's deal with the following issues:

— What Kind of Christians Do We Want To Be?

— Can We As Christians Discern What is Right and Wrong in Questionable Areas of Living?

— What are The Advantages and Disadvantages of Listening To Rock?

— What Are The Viewpoints That We Can Take Toward Rock Music?

I. What Kind of Christian Do You Want To Be?

God has promised to love us whether we listen to rock music or not. If you have trusted Jesus Christ as your personal Saviour, your standing before God in heaven is secure for all eternity. Yet, as we live day by day, all that we do affects our Christian life. So, no matter what we do, whether it be sports, studies, dating, or rock music, we must ask the question--"How does this affect my walk with God?" However, before we can even ask that question, we must ask an even more basic question, and that question is--"What kind of Christian do you want want to be?"

Three Kinds of Christians

The Bible seems to point out that there are different kinds of Christians or three different stages a Christian can be in as he/she grows to be more like Jesus Christ. These three different types of Christians are:

the "baby Christian"

the "carnal Christian"

the "maturing spiritual Christian"

A. Meet The Baby Christian

The apostle Paul in the New Testament spoke of the baby Christian:

1 Corinthians 3:1
"And I, brethren, could not speak to you as to spiritual men, but as to men of flesh, as to babes in Christ."

A baby Christian is one that has met Christ but hasn't grown up very much in the depths of knowing Him or may not know or accept what God thinks about life's issues.

Being a baby Christian does not necessarily correlate with the number of years one has been a Christian, but rather the amount of spiritual growth that has taken place in the Christian's life.

The Bible gives some of the characteristics of the attitudes and abilities and the needs of a baby Christian. A baby Christian can only understand the basic insights of Scripture.

1 Peter 2:2
"Like newborn babes, long for the pure milk of the Word, that by it you may grow in respect to salvation."

Everyone at one time or another finds himself in the baby stage of Christian growth. There is nothing wrong with being at this level of growth as long as the baby Christian keeps growing.

God does not want us to stay in the baby stage too long because when we are at that stage, we don't understand or apply very much of His Word. Since a baby Christian can only understand the basics of God's Word, it is hard for Him to know Christ very well or come to understand how God views life.

A baby Christian is also easily fooled about what is and what isn't important about life.

Ephesians 4:14 (Living Bible)
"Then we will no longer be like children, forever changing our minds about what we believe because someone has told us something different, or has cleverly lied to us and made the lie sound like the truth."

* *According to Ephesians 4:14, what is a main characteristic of the baby Christian?* ______________________

____

A BABY CHRISTIAN CAN GET CONFUSED OVER:

What is God's way versus what is the world's way.

Circumstances that come into his life.

The right way of dealing with non-Christian friends.

How to make right decisions.

Knowing what will help him or her to grow and what will not help him or her to become like Christ.

How to study the Bible.

What is true about God and what is a lie about God.

It is obvious as to why God encourages all Christians to grow out of the baby stage of the Christian life.

B. Meet the Carnal Christian

1 Corinthians 3:1-3
1) "And I, brethren, could not speak to you as to spiritual men, but as to men of flesh, as to babes in Christ.
2) "I gave you milk to drink, not solid food; for you were not yet able to receive it. Indeed, even now you are not yet able.
3) "for you are still fleshly. For since there is jealousy and strife among you, are you not fleshly, and are you not walking like mere men?"

* *According to 1 Corinthians 3:1, how must one talk to a carnal Christian?* ______________________________

* *According to 1 Corinthians 3:1-3, what is the basic problem with the carnal Christian?* ______________________________

____

* *According to 1 Corinthians 3:1-3, why is this person not a healthy Christian?* ______________________________

* *According to 1 Corinthians 3:3, how actually are these people living?* ______________________________

The carnal Christian is really a miserable person. Because he/she is out of fellowship with God, he/she cannot enjoy God. God is still at work in the carnal Christian, mostly trying to lead the one who is walking astray back into a right relationship with Him.

Although God loves us whether we are out of fellowship with Him or not, there isn't much He can do in our lives or much we can do in return to glorify Him when we are not letting Him be in control of our lives.

In Hebrews 5:11 through 14 we find Paul talking with a group of Christians about a heavy spiritual subject. He stopped talking about the deep spiritual subject because they were just too childish to pick up what he was saying. This is what He said to them:

Hebrews 5:11-14
11) "Concerning him we have much to say, and it is hard to explain, since you have become dull of hearing.
12) "For though by this time you ought to be teachers, you have need again for someone to teach you the elementary principles of the oracles of God, and you have come to need milk and not solid food.
13) "For every one who partakes only of milk is not accustomed to the word of righteousness, for he is a babe.
14) "But solid food is for the mature, who because of practice have their senses trained to discern good and evil."

*According to Hebrews 5:11-14, what are some of the problems these carnal Christians were having?

____

____

____

____

____

____

It is not God's plan for us to live like the carnal Christians described in Hebrews 5. Christians who are out of fellowship with God for long periods of time really pay a price--hours are wasted in frustration, guilt, and spiritual indifference. It is obvious that God in no way wants us to go on living in a state of being carnal. But the fact remains that many students remain out of fellowship with God.

C. Meet the Maturing Christian

Who is the Maturing Spirit-Filled Christian?

He is the Christian who makes pleasing God the single most important priority in his life. This person, although sometimes failing, wants God to be in complete control of his life. His life is marked by seeking after God and his obedience toward God.

Paul talks about this type of Christian in:

Philippians 1:9-11
9) "And this I pray, that your love may abound still more and more in real knowledge and all discernment,
10) "so that you may approve the things that are excellent, in order to be sincere and blameless until the day of Christ;
11) "having been filled with the fruit of righteousness which comes through Jesus Christ, to the glory and praise of God."

In the verses Phil. 1:9-11 let's pick out the marks of a maturing Christian?

He is increasing in love. *This person is learning to love others in a deeper more consistant way.*

He is receiving more spiritual knowledge. *This person is learning more and more about God.*

He is acquiring more discernment. *This person is able to more and more distinguish between right and wrong.*

He is increasing in sincerity. *This person is learning to have purer motives in all that he/she does.*

The great thing about a maturing Christian is that he is not asking "what can I get away with before God" but rather "what can I do to please God." This person seeks to find out what God wants and quickly does it. It is to the maturing or Spirit-filled Christian that God promises the fulfillment of the Christian life.

Listening to rock music does not necessarily make us a baby Christian, carnal Christian, or a maturing Christian. It does, however, have an influence on us in our walk with Jesus. Since this is true, we must then ask ourselves the questions--

In what way does rock music affect us?

What kind of a Christian do we want to be?

II. DOES GOD GIVE US THE ABILITY TO DISTINGUISH BETWEEN WHAT DOES AND WHAT DOES NOT PLEASE HIM?

God wants us to be able to distinguish between what is good for us and that which will ultimately do us harm. He does not want us in any way to be confused about any area of our life. In his Word He gives hundreds of verses on how we should live to please Him and therefore make our lives fulfilled in Him. He also gives us guidelines from the Scripture so that we can apply them to specific areas of our lives. These guidelines apply to rock and roll music as well.

For example He says in:

Proverbs 2:2-7
2) "Make your ear attentive to wisdom, incline your heart to understanding;
3) "For if you cry for discernment, lift your voice for understanding;
4) "If you seek her as silver, and search for her as for hidden treasures;
5) "Then you will discern the fear of the Lord, and discover the knowledge of God.
6) "For the Lord gives wisdom; from His mouth come knowledge and understanding.
7) "He stores up sound wisdom for the upright; He is a shield to those who walk in integrity."

Scripture	Scripture Applied To Rock
Proverbs 2:2-7	
Make your ear attentive to wisdom	*Be willing to hear God's point of view on rock music.*
Incline your ear to understanding	*Be willing to respond to rock music the way God wants you to.*
For if you cry for discernment	*If you say to God, "Lord, please help me to know what is right and wrong about rock."*
Lift your voice for understanding	*If you say, "Lord, help me to accept and think about the whole "rock world" the way you do."*
If you seek her as silver and search for hidden treasure	*If you really want to know what the Lord wants for you with all your heart, even in the areas of rock music,*
Then you will discern the fear of the Lord	*then you will know what it is to have deep respect and love for the Lord.*
And discover the knowledge of God	*And then you will see the tremendous wisdom and insights God has for you.*

Now that we have asked the preliminary question as to what kind of Christian God wants us to be, and have discovered that we can know what is good and evil, let us now look at the "pros and cons" of rock music.

God tells us that if we want to know what is right and wrong about life around us, He will surely show us. The Bible speaks of this in:

Hebrews 5:14
"But solid food is for the mature, who because of practice have their senses trained to discern good and evil."

* *According to Hebrews 5:14, how does the maturing Christian learn to discern between good and evil?* __________

____

Ways to Discern Good and Evil

Here are some activities and questions. We can ask God and check out His Word to find out if what we are doing is pleasing to God.

We can look directly in the Word of God and see if Scripture supports or warns against the activity.

We can be so led by the Holy Spirit that He will bear witness to our conscience, whether or not we can be involved in that particular activity. God does lead us through the Spirit to all truth (John 16:13).

We can ask if the particular activity helps or hurts our walk with Jesus.

We can ask if the particular activity is bigger in our life than God is.

We can watch other people who are into the activity to see what effect it has on them.

THE ADVANTAGES OF LISTENING TO ROCK

COUNTER-ARGUMENT AGAINST LISTENING TO ROCK MUSIC

In the following section of this chapter on "rock" we want to (as clearly as possible) put the opposing viewpoints on the pros and cons of listening to "rock music".

ROCK MUSIC IS POPULAR AND I ENJOY IT

Rock is popular with most all of my friends. Rock is so popular it is often the focal point for conversation and enjoyment. Most parties have rock music as its main thrust. It's sort of something everyone can get into together at a party or a dance. Besides there is a whole life-style that comes from the rock scene; it's a life-style in which I want to be identified.

POPULARITY HAS NOTHING TO DO WITH IT

Simply because rock is popular, is not that good of reason to get into it. The question worth asking is with whom is it popular and why is it popular? Sin, for example, is popular (everyone does it) but that doesn't mean God wants Christians to do it.

So what that there's a whole life style around rock and rock stars, it's not the kind of life-style I'd want to follow anyway, for the most part the kind of culture that comes out of the whole rock scene is Godless anyway.

Rock Music Keeps My Mind From Getting Bored

I actually don't spend that much time listening to rock. I usually only listen to it while I'm doing something else, like driving the car, cleaning the house, or doing my homework. It helps to keep my mind from becoming bored.

So, listening to rock livens up my life and it isn't that time consuming.

God Wants Us To Use Our Time Wisely

In some ways rock music can be helpful in keeping your mind from getting bored, but rock music also has it's void and God has better alternatives to it.

God teaches us in the Bible that time is an important commodity and we should use it wisely. If we can do two things at the same time, then it is obviously a good idea to do so. The question remains-- Is there something more profitable things we could be doing with our mind than listening to secular rock music? For example, why not spend more time listening to Jesus music?

God clearly wants to use music in our lives. He says in:

Colossians 3:16-17
16) "Let the word of Christ richly dwell within you, with all wisdom teaching and admonishing one another with psalms and hymns and spiritual songs, singing with thankfulness in your hearts to God.
17) "And whatever you do in word or deed, do all in the name of the Lord Jesus, giving thanks through Him to God the Father."

Many people love music and you must be one of them, so let God's music fill your mind. Get a tape deck in your car and begin to collect good Jesus music.

God also asks us to be in an attitude of prayer. God commands us to pray without ceasing. Maybe if you used that "boring" time as a prayer time, your life would take on new meaning and purpose. Try taping a prayer list over your car radio, a list that has the names of people that need your prayers. When you reach over to

GOD WANTS US TO USE OUR TIME WISELY CONT'D

turn on your favorite rock station let that list remind you to pray those people. (If you are driving car it would be wise to keep your eyes open while you pray.)

There are so many other things we could be doing other than being addicted to rock music. God no doubt would rather you choose the best things and do them.

PROJECT

HOW MUCH DO I REALLY LISTEN TO ROCK MUSIC?

Make a tabulation of how much time you spend listening to rock radio, records, going to secular concerts or reading about rock stars. Then tabulate how much time you spend with God in the Word, prayer or having Christ centered fellowship with other Christians. This should give you some indication as to what is in reality important to you and where your time is going.

Rock Music Helps Me To Have Compassion Towards Non-Christians

As a Christian I need to listen to rock music to better understand the world in which I live. When I listen to some of the lyrics of the songs, I realize how non-Christians think and it helps me to be more compassionate to the people who do not know Christ.

There are other Ways to Get Compassion

It is good to want to be compassionate and help the lost world in which we live. It is also important to understand the way that non-Christians think. But the real questions come down to how much rock do we need to listen to before we understand the non-Christian? How much rock do we need to consume before we know that many non-Christians are hung up in selfishness, loneliness, purposelessness, misuse of drugs and alcohol or sex.

God's Word already tells us what most people are thinking in this modern age.

The danger for the Christian is that we may start out listening to rock music to get a better understanding of our culture but end up hooked on the very music that puts forth Godless values.

I JUST LISTEN TO THE BEAT

People are always talking about how bad or dirty many lyrics to rock songs are, but I don't listen to the words,-- I just like the beat.

MANY OF THE ROCK LYRICS ARE AGAINST GOD'S WAYS AND WHETHER YOU KNOW IT OR NOT YOU ARE AFFECTED BY THEM

Just a casual glance at many rock songs should alert us to their non-Christlike ways of thinking. Your mind is an amazing mechanism, the human brain picks up and stores in it's subconscious all it hears; consequently if you are listening to Godless lyrics your subconscious is storing them and they could influence you against God's ways.

For example, there is an old hit song by the rock group, "The Eagles", called Take It Easy. The words of this song tell us all we have to do is lie back and not be concerned about life's responsibilities. That we should not even try to understand others, just worry about yourself and don't do anything. Let's see what God says about that thought in:

Proverbs 6:9-11
9) "How long will you lie down, O sluggard? When will you arise from your sleep?
10) "A little sleep, a little slumber, a little folding of the hands to rest--
11) "And your poverty will come in like a vagabond, and your need like an armed man."

✱ What do you think would happen to a person if he followed the advice that the song Take It Easy tells us to? ____________

____

Let's Take Another Example

Another hit song recorded a while back by a female recording star, Mary McGregor, called Torn Between Two Lovers, also gives us a worldly way of looking at things. This song seems to imply that the girl can have two lovers at the same time. She goes on to say that she knows she is breaking the rules but that is OK with her. She also mentions a void in her life that can only be filled with sex. The lyrics of that song tell us a lot about a certain value system that is godless. It is basically saying that we can make up our own rules. We can live as we please, doing what we want. Good is what I say good is.

This point of view about life and its values goes against what God says in the Bible.

Isaiah 5:20
"Woe to those who call evil good, and good evil; who substitute darkness for light and light for darkness; who substitute bitter for sweet, and sweet for bitter!"

We must ask ourselves--What kind of thoughts do we want spreading into our conscious and subconscious mind? Do we want thoughts that keep us from thinking about the Lord, or put into our sub-conscious thoughts that are godless?

The Bible teaches us that our thought life is so important in our walk with God.

Some lyrics are harmless in what they say, while others are downright dangerous to our Christian life. As Christians, can we risk what raunchy lyrics will do to our minds and lives?

The two songs mentioned are now outdated. But following is a project that will help you to rate the popular songs of today.

PROJECT

RATING ROCK SONGS

Get the lyrics of the top 20 songs on the charts and rate them the following way:

* *This song blatently goes against God and His Word. (Tell how and show Scripture to prove it.)*

* *This song subtly puts forth an attitude or thought that goes against God and His ways.*

* *This song is just a love song and is more or less harmless.*

* *This song actually makes statements that God says are true. Use Scripture to show this.*

* *This song helps me have more compassion toward the non-Christian or more love for God.*

IV. Here are some viewpoints towards rock that we can take

After looking at the type of Christian you want to be and weighing the pros and cons of listening to rock music, you need to make a decision on what you will do with rock music.

There are basically only three options from which you have to choose.

A. The—I won't listen to rock music at all option

The reasons for this viewpoint are:

___ *It's time consuming.*

___ *I don't want my conscious and subconscious mind muddled with useless and Godless values put forth by the lyrics in rock music.*

___ *I want more time to pray, study the Word, and fellowship with other Christians.*

___ *I don't like the whole life-style which rock stars seem to promote.*

___ *I like music, but there's plenty of Jesus music that is much better for me.*

___ *I just don't like rock music.*

If you hold to this viewpoint, check the reasons as to why you don't listen to it.

B. The—I want to keep on listening to rock music a lot option

The reasons for this viewpoint are:

___ *I like rock music, especially the beat.*

___ *The words don't really affect me in a negative way.*

___ *I know God loves me and will keep working in my life anyway.*

___ *My friends like rock and I want to have this in common with them.*

___ *I can identify with a lot of the songs.*

___ *Most Christian songs don't match up to the musical quality of secular rock.*

If you hold to this viewpoint, check the reasons as to why you want to keep on listening to rock music.

C. The—I Want to Be a Selective Listener Option

The reasons for this viewpoint are:

___ *I like rock but I don't want to be controlled by it.*

___ *I realize that some lyrics are bad for me in that they could affect my conscious and subconscious mind.*

___ *I listen to the lyrics once and if I consider them Godless I either turn off the radio or turn to another station whenever the song comes on.*

___ *I try to balance the time I spend listening to secular music by spending the equivalent of time listening to Jesus music.*

___ *I can take or leave rock music.*

___ *The more I get to know Jesus, the less I care about secular music.*

If you hold to this viewpoint, check the reasons as to why you don't listen to it.

In Conclusion

God wants us to have a clear conscience in all that we do. He wants us to enjoy life to its fullest. The way that we enjoy life to its fullest is to live life His way. He tells us His way in His Word.

God wants us to think about at least three different thoughts from His Word as we make up our minds about rock music.

Can I Glorify Christ by Listening to Rock?

Colossians 3:17
"And whatever you do in word or deed, do all in the name of the Lord Jesus, giving thanks through Him to God the Father."

How am I Using My Time?

Ephesians 5:15-17
15) "Therefore be careful how you walk, not as unwise men, but as wise,
16) "making the most of your time, because the days are evil.
17) "So then do not be foolish, but understand what the will of the Lord is."

What Has Control of Me?

M

1 Corinthians 6:12
"All things are lawful for me, but not all things are profitable. All things are lawful for me, but I will not be mastered by anything."

As mentioned earlier, God's love remains constant whether you listen to rock music or not. You must decide for yourself whether you do glorify God by listening to rock music; if you are making the best use of your time by listening, buying and talking about rock; and if God is in control of your life by listening to rock.

Only you can decide if you want to be a baby Christian, carnal Christian, or a maturing, Spirit-filled Christian.

NOTES

Disciplining your TIME

IN TODAY'S FAST MOVING SOCIETY, THERE IS NOTHING WE WASTE MORE THAN TIME.

We know that because of its qualities, time is an amazing phenomenon. It cannot be stretched, stored, stopped, or even slowed down. God is not restricted by time, but He has set up minutes, hours, and days for man to use freely.

However, time on this earth has its limits. God has appointed a set amount of days for every man. It is safe to say that time is one of the most precious commodities we have. Since time is so important, God wants every man to use his few short moments on this earth in the most meaningful and responsible way possible. We need to be continually petitioning God, along with the psalmist:

Psalm 90:12
"Teach us to number our days, that we may present to Thee a heart of wisdom."

Since the way you manage your time is so important to God, let's examine:

I. WRONG WAYS OF SPENDING TIME

II. HOW GOD WANTS YOU TO SPEND YOUR TIME

III. HOW TO DISCIPLINE YOUR TIME

I. THERE ARE MANY WRONG WAYS FOR MAN TO SPEND HIS TIME

Since man is so sinful, and time allows such freedom, a person can easily find ways to waste time. There has never been anyone who has wasted more time than Satan. Most of his time has been spent hindering the work of God. It is Satan's desire that man spend his hours doing anything other than thinking and acting upon the person of Jesus Christ. Satan wants Christians to waste their time, so that in no way can they honor God or lead another to Jesus Christ.

Here are just a few examples of how we, as Christians, can be tricked into wasting time.

ONE WAY WE WASTE TIME IS BY BEING LAZY

A. What is Laziness?

1. Laziness is the habit of being wasteful with time because of an unmotivated or undisciplined attitude toward life.

God shows us a number of problems the lazy man has.

Proverbs 6:6-11
6) "Go to the ant, O sluggard, observe her ways and be wise,
7) "which, having no chief, officer, or ruler,
8) "prepares her food in the summer, and gathers her provisions in the harvest.
9) "How long will you lie down, O sluggard? When will you arise from your sleep?
10) "A little sleep, a little slumber, a little folding of the hands to rest,
11) "and your poverty will come in like a vagabond, and your need like an armed man."

* *According to verses 6-8, the ant has two qualities that the lazy person refuses to obtain. What are they?*

____

____

The ant has no one forcing him to work, but he is extremely motivated to accomplish his task. The lazy man, on the other hand, will only work when someone is standing right over him; and even then, he is usually working with the wrong attitude. An employer will soon fire a person like this since it's impossible for him to be watching his employee every minute of the day.

* *According to Proverbs 6:6-8, what other quality does the ant have that is not characteristic of the lazy man?*

____

____

Not only is the ant highly motivated and hard working, but he also refuses to procrastinate. He continually plans ahead for the future.

2. Laziness is the Habit of Procrastination

Circle some of the things you tend to put off.

- *Homework*
- *Jobs your parents want you do do*
- *Getting up in the morning*
- *Writing letters*
- *Returning library books*
- *Getting a job*
- *Apologizing to a person*
- *Paying back money you owe*
- *Fulfilling promises*
- ______________________
- ______________________
- ______________________

The procrastinator continually fools himself because he visualizes himself succeeding when he never really does the work. One day, he wakes up and finds it is too late to do the job -- and his negligence has caused irrepairable damage.

Proverbs 6:9-11
9) "How long will you lie down, O sluggard? When will you arise from your sleep?
10) "A little sleep, a little slumber, a little folding of the hands to rest,
11) "and your poverty will come in like a vagabond, and your need like an armed man."

3. Laziness is the Habit of Being a Sluggard

* *According to Proverbs 6:9-11, what is a sluggard?*

He is one who has a problem with oversleeping. Although sleep is something he can't live without -- and some people need more of it than others -- the lazy man completely overdoes it. The lazy man has a difficult time facing up to reality, and so he uses oversleeping as an escape mechanism. He finds great pleasure in doing nothing. Consequently, his main exercise for the day is rolling over in bed.

Proverbs 26:14
"As the door turns on its hinges, so does the sluggard on his bed."

* *According to Proverbs 6:10-11, what is the main frustration of the lazy man?*

____

____

____

The greatest frustration of the lazy man is that, while he has big dreams, he is suddenly hit with the necessities of life. So, he has two frustrations hitting him at once. He has developed the habit of laziness and, therefore, hates work. But, at the same time, he is hurting because of his poor situation. Consequently, the lazy man not only wastes time God has given him, but also finds himself in continual frustration.

> *It is obvious to see that wasting time by being lazy is not God's way to happiness and success.*

Proverbs 13:4
"The soul of the sluggard craves and gets nothing, but the soul of the diligent is made fat."

B. ANOTHER WAY WE WASTE TIME IS BY HAVING THE WRONG PRIORITIES

An example of wasting time comes when we become too involved with chasing things that really don't matter.

1. Nice Activities

Because time allows us to much freedom we, as Christians, have almost limitless ways in which to spend it. The trick Satan uses is to get us involved in activities that are nice but do not accomplish God's will, or do anything that will count for eternity. God gives us many wonderful things to do in life, but He does not want us to waste large segments of our time chasing His gifts rather than Him.

King David understood this thought very well when he wrote:

Psalm 39:4-7

4) "Lord, make me to know my end, and what is the extent of my days, let me know how transient I am.

5) "Behold, Thou hast made my days as handbreadths, and my life time as nothing in Thy sight, surely every man at his best is a mere breath.

6) "Surely every man walks about as a phantom; surely they make an uproar for nothing; he amasses riches, and does not know who will gather them.

7) "And now, Lord, for what do I wait? My hope is in Thee."

2. Material Dreams

For example, the Christian who spends his time chasing after material dreams -- rather than the things God says are important -- is simply wasting his and God's time. The reason for this is that time is spent gathering material objects that soon fall apart.

Jesus showed what a waste of time this type of activity really is, when He said:

Matthew 6:19-20
19) "Do not lay up for yourselves treasures upon earth, where moth and rust destroy, and where thieves break in and steal.
20) "But lay up for yourselves treasures in heaven, where neither moth nor rust destroys, and where thieves do not break in and steal."

Can you think of some activities that are not wrong in themselves but, if overdone, will waste God's time and, therefore, grieve Him?

FOR EXAMPLE:

- *Watching television*
- *Driving your car*
- *Studying*
- *Riding horses*
- *Cooking*
- *Athletics*
- *Hunting*
- *Sewing*
- *Cleaning the house*
- *Girlfriends/boyfriends*
- *Sleeping*
- *Eating*
- *Listening to the radio*
- *Spending time with friends*

3. Eternal Perspective

God wants you to look at life from an eternal perspective. He realizes that while your life here on earth is just a speck in time, what you do in that time greatly affects what will happen in eternity.

Everything you do should have an eternal perspective. When you glorify God (see Chapter 1), you are continually using your time effectively for eternity. That is why it is silly to spend your time doing anything unless God is completely involved in the activity with you. Though you may spend large amounts of time in hard work, if God does not have complete control of the time, it is wasted.

Psalm 127:1-2 (Living Bible)

1) "Unless the Lord builds a house, the builders' work is useless. Unless the Lord protects a city, sentries do no good.

2) "It is senseless for you to work so hard from early morning until late at night, fearing you will starve to death; for God wants His loved ones to get their proper rest."

II. How God Wants You to Spend Your Time

Since time is so important, God -- in His Word -- graciously reveals to you some guidelines that will help you spend your time wisely.

A. GOD WANTS YOU TO PLAN YOUR LIFESTYLE KNOWING THAT TIME IS RUNNING OUT

Ephesians 5:15-18

15) "Therefore be careful how you walk, not as unwise men, but as wise,

16) "making the most of your time, because the days are evil.

17) "So then do not be foolish, but understand what the will of the Lord is.

18) "And do not get drunk with wine, for that is dissipation, but be filled with the Spirit."

* *According to verse 15, how can you tell a wise man from an unwise man?*

____

* *According to verse 16, for what reason does God ask you to make the most of your time?*

____

* *According to verse 17, what is the guideline you should use in making good use of your time?*

____

* *According to verse 18, where do you get the power to make good use of your time, understand God's will, and be careful how you live?*

____

____

God points out that the Christian won't waste his time if he helps another Christian become more like Jesus Christ.

Hebrews 10:24-25

24) "And let us consider how to stimulate one another to love and good deeds,

25) "not forsaking our own assembling together, as is the habit of some, but encouraging one another; and all the more, as you see the day drawing near."

* *According to verse 25, why are we to encourage and warn one another?*

____

____

B. GOD SEES TIME RUNNING OUT HERE ON EARTH

Jesus Christ was a man who saw the urgency of the hour. The amazing thing about Jesus Christ is that He was always on time and never wasted it. He summed up why we should use our time wisely, when He said:

John 9:4
"We must work the works of Him who sent Me, as long as it is day; night is coming, when no man can work."

C. ANOTHER WAY YOU CAN MAKE GOOD USE OF YOUR TIME IS TO BE INVOLVED IN ACTIVITIES THAT WILL LENGTHEN YOUR DAYS

God knows that every minute of your life can be crucial and affect all of eternity. Since this is so, He only wants you to do things that will add years to your life -- rather than take them away.

Sin, which causes anxiety, takes a great toll on our days here on earth. Rebellion toward God will not only make your time on earth miserable, but it can also shorten your life. Of course, sin is not the only reason why some die early. God, in His sovereignty, allows some people to die before others. Yet, as a general rule, we will enjoy a longer life if we follow God's guidelines for living.

Psalm 34:12-14
12) "Who is the man who desires life, and loves length of days
that he may see good?
13) "Keep your tongue from evil, and your lips from speaking
deceit.
14) "Depart from evil, and do good; seek peace, and pursue it."

* According to the above verses, what are some guidelines that God wants you to follow if you want a long and fulfilling life?

____

____

* Why do you think doing these things will give you a long and fulfilled life?

____

God will bless you for obeying His guidelines, and you will escape the consequences of sin (guilt, anxiety, fear, etc.), which are killers.

God gives man a command to obey, if he wants to enjoy a long and good life on earth.

Ephesians 6:1-3
1) "Children, obey your parents in the Lord, for this is right.
2) "Honor your father and mother (which is the first commandment with a promise),
3) "that it may be well with you and that you may live long on the earth."

* *According to verse 3, what does God promise you if you obey and honor your parents?*

____

God wants you to avoid the results of disobeying your parents.

* *What are some of the problems you would encounter if you ignored God's command?*

____

____

____

God loves you so much that He has given His commands and guidelines to prolong your life and make it more enjoyable. He urges you to make good use of your time, by following them and avoiding activities that will only hurt you and draw you away from Him. He promises you:

1 Kings 3:14
"And if you walk in My ways, keeping My statutes and commandments, as your father David walked, then I will prolong your days."

III. How to Discipline Your Time

To get the most out of your day for God, you should take several steps.

A. The First Step in Using Your Time Wisely Is to Set Specific Goals for Yourself

One of the biggest reasons you have difficulty using your time wisely is that you haven't decided what God wants you to do with the time you have. Jesus Christ never had this problem. He knew exactly how God wanted Him to spend His time on earth, and He focused His efforts on doing those things. This enabled Him to make this statement:

John 7:14
"I glorified Thee on the earth, having accomplished the work which Thou hast given Me to do."

The Bible says that Jesus spent time growing in four important areas of His life.

Luke 2:52
"And Jesus kept increasing in wisdom and stature, and in favor with God and men."

1) *Wisdom - Intellectually*

2) *Stature - Physically*

3) *Favor with God - Spiritually*

4) *Favor with men - Socially*

A TIMELY PROJECT

Take 15 minutes to do the following:

Ask God to show you some specific goals that you could work toward in each of the four areas listed in Luke 2:52.

On a sheet of paper, under each area, state what your goals are, how you are going to reach them, and when you are going to spend time working toward them.

Your paper might look something like this:

MY GOALS FOR THE NEXT SEMESTER ARE

WISDOM *(INTELLECT)*

Goal: to get at least a "B" in my chemistry class
How I will accomplish it: I will study chemistry for at least 45 minutes a day.
When will I do this? Monday through Thursday evenings, from 9:00 - 9:45 p.m.

STATURE *(PHYSICAL)*

Goal: to stay in good physical condition and improve my tennis game
How I will accomplish it: I will play tennis three times a week for 1 1/2 hours.
When will I do this? Monday - Wednesday - Friday afternoons, from 3:00 - 4:30 p.m.

FAVOR WITH GOD *(SPIRITUAL)*

Goal: to have a daily time alone with God, reading the Bible and praying.
How I will accomplish it: I will discipline myself to get up a half hour earlier until it becomes a habit.
When will I do this? Every morning, from 6:30 - 7:00 a.m.

FAVOR WITH MEN *(SOCIAL)*

Goal: to take more time to talk and do things with my parents.
How I will accomplish it: I will take at least an hour in the evenings with them and make my family more of a priority in my life.
When will I do this? In the evenings, from 6:30 - 7:30 p.m., and on weekends.

It is very important to be specific and practical when you list your goals. Don't be afraid to challenge yourself when you are deciding on them. Trusting God in these areas will help you to grow in your faith. Setting goals will help you use your time to accomplish worthwhile things.

B. The Second Step in Using Our Time Wisely Is to Discover How We Can Make Better Use of the Time We Have

Another Timely Project

Take another 15 minutes to do the following:

List all your weekly activities, then determine the hours spent on each activity. Your list might look like this:

How I Spend My Time

Activities	*Hours*
School	*35*
Sleep	*56*
Eating	*11*
Watching TV	*15*
Studying	*10*
Church	*4*
Dates	*5*
Bible study	*2*
Talking on the phone	*5*

From your list, determine the activities that are wasting your time, or if you are spending too much time in a certain activity. For example, if you are spending 15 hours a week watching TV, or 5 hours on the phone with friends, perhaps you should consider how you could make better use of that time. If you cut back watching TV to 5 hours a week, you will have an extra 10 hours to do more important things -- such as spending time with your family, studying, or in a Bible study.

It is important for your to find your priorities in life, then focus your time and energy on them. Not to do so is to waste valuable time which could be spent on activities that would have a positive effect on your life.

C. THE FINAL STEP IN USING YOUR TIME WISELY IS TO MAKE A SCHEDULE OF ALL YOUR WEEKLY ACTIVITIES

Have you ever had one of the following experiences?

It's 12 o'clock at night when suddenly you wake up in a cold sweat. You've just remembered you haven't studied for an important history test you have the next day.

Or, have you ever had one of these experiences?

You accepted a date for the same night you were supposed to babysit for the neighbors, and didn't realize it until you saw your date standing at the front door.

You forgot that you promised your younger sister a day at the park, and you made plans to go sailing with your friends. Your sister asks you if you are ready to go, just as you are walking out the door to meet your friends.

It is extremely important to know what activities you will be involved in during the week, and when you will do them. For this reason, it's handy to write out a schedule for your week. A schedule is a record of what, and when, you will be doing things that week.

STILL ANOTHER PROJECT!

Take a sheet of paper and make it into a schedule like the example below:

	Monday	Tuesday	Wednesday	Thursday	Friday	Saturday	Sunday
6							
8							
10							
12							
2							
4							
6							
8							
10							
12							

Next, shade in the time slots when you are doing set activities that can't be changed. (Things like school, sleeping, job, etc.) Then, add the activities that must be done that week. Don't forget your goals! Activities such as studying for that history test. Shade them in at the most logical times possible. (Hint: Don't schedule study time on Friday for the test you have Thursday!)

Finally, shade in any other activities you have in order of their importance. Your schedule may look something like this:

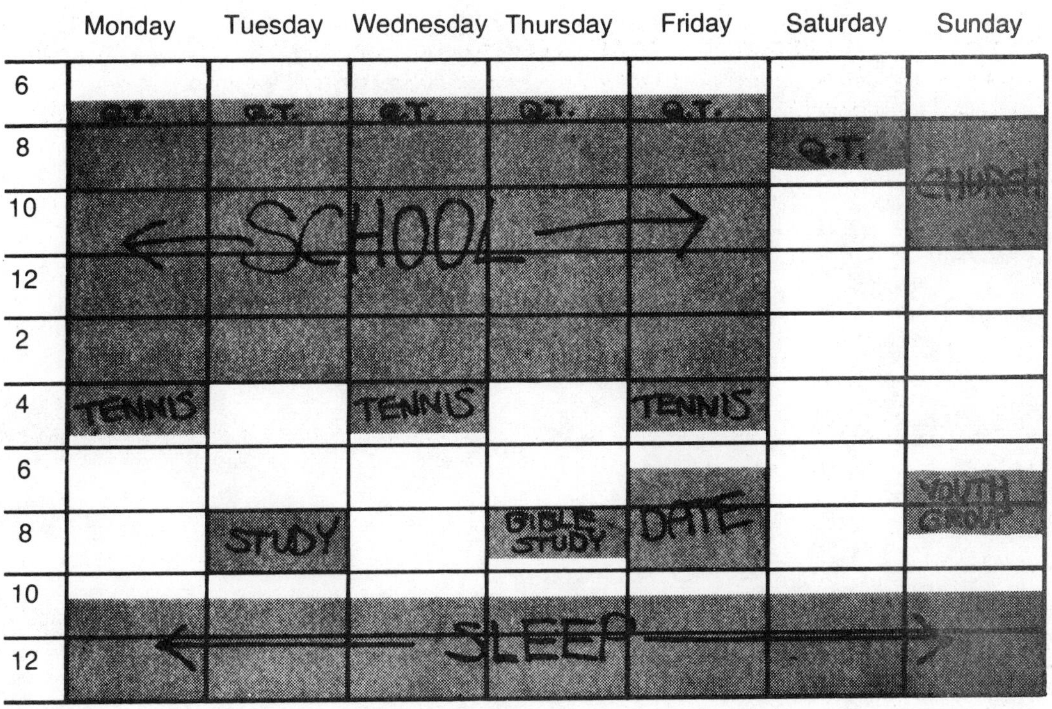
Monday
Tuesday
Wednesday
Thursday
Friday
Saturday
Sunday
6
8
10
12
2
4
6
8
10
12
Q.T.
Q.T.
Q.T.
Q.T.
Q.T.
Q.T.
CHURCH
SCHOOL
TENNIS
TENNIS
TENNIS
STUDY
BIBLE STUDY
DATE
YOUTH GROUP
SLEEP

A schedule will help you determine when your free time is, and will help motivate you to use your time wisely. Using a schedule as a tool to help manage your time better will result in accomplishing more. Suggestion: Your parents might like to know what you're up to! Give them a copy of your schedule.

It is very important for you, as a Christian, to spend your time doing things that will count for eternity. Wasting time is not God's desire for your life. He wants you to make the best possible use of your time -- by disciplining yourself to do the things that are important in His eyes.

Setting goals and scheduling your time are two ways to make sure you use your time wisely for God. Time can be used for accomplishing important, worthwhile things, or it can be misused. How you use your time will greatly affect the outcome of your life.

How to face DEATH

ONE PHENOMENA THAT EVERY PERSON HAS IN COMMON WITH ANOTHER IS THE AWESOME EVENT OF DEATH

There is probably no subject which causes more confusion, fear, and sorrow than dying. Most people either try to avoid the thoughts of dying, or so cover it up that it seems to be pushed far from their minds. But, even when one tries to avoid thinking of death, he must, sooner or later, face the fact that he must die.

God declared that all men must die, when He said:

Hebrews 9:27
"And, inasmuch as it is appointed for man to die once, and after this comes judgment."

The Bible teaches that every man (unless he is a Christian when Christ returns) will one day be lowered six feet under -- with his body soon turning to dust. Since God shows no partiality with any man, no amount of status, fame, money, or power will be able to stop man from "walking through the valley of the shadow of death".

King Solcmon, the wisest man in the Bible, understood this thought when he wrote:

Ecclesiastes 2:16
"For there is no lasting remembrance of the wise man as with the fool, inasmuch as in the coming days all will be forgotten. And how the wise man and the fool alike die!"

Later King Solomon wrote:

Ecclesiastes 5:15-16

15) "As he had come naked from his mother's womb, so will he return as he came. He will take nothing from the fruit of his labor that he can carry in his hand.

16) "And there also is a grievous evil -- exactly as a man is born, thus will he die. So, what is the advantage to him who toils for the wind?"

In spite of the fact that every man will someday have to face eternity, few really understand the deep implications of death and what one can expect when he dies. Even among Christians, confusion and fear over death is the rule, rather than the exception. God in no way wants His children to be confused or fearful about dying. He explains the subject of death in His Word so that no Christian should be alarmed.

SINCE DEATH IS SUCH AN OVERWHELMING SUBJECT, LET'S TRY TO UNDERSTAND. . .

I. What Death Is

II. Why There Is Death

III. What God Has Done About Dying

IV. Where One Goes When He Dies

I. What is Death?

Since dying is such a spiritual phenomena, many people are confused as to what death actually means. They stand by a casket and know that something is wrong -- it's obvious that a body is not designed to function without a soul -- but they can't always figure out what has taken place.

God, meanwhile, wants us all to understand what death involves. He says:

1 Thessalonians 4:13
"But we do not want you to be uninformed, brethren, about those who are asleep, that you may not grieve, as do the rest who have no hope."

DEATH BASICALLY MEANS SEPARATION, OR WRONG EXISTENCE, BUT CAN APPLY TO THESE DIFFERENT SITUATIONS:

A. Physical Death

Which is when man's soul and spirit are separated from his body

B. Spiritual Death

In which a person is still alive but living a life apart from God and is, therefore, living in wrong existence

C. Eternal Death

Which is the total separation of man from God -- man is banished by God to eternal punishment.

A. What is Physical Death?

THE BIBLE'S DESCRIPTION OF PHYSICAL DEATH . . .

Throughout the pages of Scripture, we find examples of when a man's soul and spirit depart and leave his body. Nowhere in the Bible, however, does it teach that a man's soul and spirit go out of existence.

Job, writing in one of the oldest books of the Bible, stated:

Job 19:25-26
25) "Even as for me, I know that my Redeemer lives, and at the last He will take His stand on the earth.
26) "Even after my skin is flayed, yet without my flesh, I shall see God."

To understand death more clearly, we must understand that we are made up of more than just a body. The Bible explains to us that our being consists of a Body, Soul, and Spirit.

1 Thessalonians 5:23
"Now may the God of peace Himself sanctify you entirely; and may your spirit and soul and body be preserved complete, without blame at the coming of our Lord Jesus Christ."

FOR EXAMPLE:

THE BODY

is the visible part of man that touches the material world through its five senses: sight, smell, touch, taste, and hearing.

THE SOUL

is the part of man that functions but is invisible. It includes man's emotions, conscience, memory, and reasoning power.

THE SPIRIT

gets its feelings and insights through the soul. But, its main objective is to deal with the spiritual. The spiritual elements with which it deals include faith, reverence, worship, prayer, etc.

When a man dies, the invisible part of him -- soul and spirit -- leave his body.

A good biblical example of the soul and spirit leaving the body at the time of physical death is recorded at the death of Stephen. Stephen, a great man of God, infuriated a sinful and angry mob with his powerful preaching. The Bible tells us that while they were stoning him to death, the following events took place:

Acts 7:57-60

57) "But they cried out with a loud voice, and covered their ears, and they rushed upon him with one impulse.

58) "And when they had driven him out of the city, they began stoning him, and the witnesses laid aside their robes at the feet of a young man named Saul.

59) "And they went on stoning Stephen as he called upon the Lord and said, 'Lord Jesus, receive my spirit!'

60) "And falling on his knees, he cried out with a loud voice, 'Lord, do not hold this sin against them!' And having said this, he fell asleep."

All men have something in common with Stephen. While we may not die as dramatically or cruelly as he did, our spirit does leave our body and go somewhere else at the time of death.

B. WHAT IS SPIRITUAL DEATH?

SPIRITUAL DEATH IS . . .

. . . the condition in which all unbelievers find themselves. It is the separation of their souls from God while they are still living on this earth.

God is the very source of life and abundant living. When man cut himself off from God and His holiness, he separated himself from the source and power for real living.

Paul explained this to the church of Ephesus when he wrote:

Ephesians 2:1-2
1) "And you were dead in your trespasses and sin,
2) "in which you formerly walked according to the course of this world, according to the prince of the power of the air, of the spirit that is now working in the sons of disobedience."

* *Even though the people Paul was talking about were alive, what does he say (in verse 1) they really were?*

____

* *According to verse 2, what are some of the things they were doing that caused them to be spiritually dead?*

____

____

The Bible, speaking of a woman who was living an immoral life, explains that even a living person can be spiritually dead.

1 Timothy 5:6
"But she who gives herself to wanton pleasure is dead even while she lives."

HERE ARE SOME SIGNS OF SPIRITUAL DEATH

- *Rebellious attitude toward God*
- *A lack of understanding of spiritual things*
- *Pride*
- *Indifference toward others*
- *A life seeking pleasure rather than God*
- *Selfishness*
- *Living only for today*
- *Love of money over God*
- *Hating authority*
- *Etc. - the list is endless*

C. WHAT IS ETERNAL DEATH?

ETERNAL DEATH IS BY FAR . . .

. . . the saddest of all the deaths. It is what takes place when God banishes the non-believer from His presence forever -- dooming this person to judgment for all eternity.

Nothing could be more tragic for the unbeliever than to stand before God and be judged for his unbelief in Christ. This person, the Bible says, will be sentenced to a life of total separation from God and banished to an existence of destruction in hell.

The Apostle Paul spoke of how awful this death is when he said:

2 Thessalonians 1:9
"And these will pay the penalty of eternal destruction, away from the presence of the Lord and from the glory of His power."

The Bible teaches that the unbeliever's soul will live on forever, but he will suffer terrible misery and heartbreak.

Speaking about this, God says:

Revelation 21:8
"But for the cowardly and unbelieving and abominable and murderers and immoral persons and sorcerers and idolaters and all liars, their part will be in the lake that burns with fire and brimstone, which is the second death."

THE ONLY DEATH THAT A PERSON REALLY HAS TO EXPERIENCE...

. . . is physical death. For the one who experiences spiritual and eternal death, there is only tragedy awaiting him forever. When sin is viewed from an eternal perspective, its awfulness becomes apparent. No matter what sin can offer man in this life, it can only ruin him for eternity.

II. WHY IS THERE DEATH?

A. SIN, THE KILLER

There is no question that death is an awful phenomena. Jesus Christ went to the funeral of his friend, Lazarus, and wept over the cause and consequences of dying. God hates death with all His being. If death is absolute wrong existence, then why has God allowed death to come to man? Death is the price that all men must pay for rebelling against God. God hates sin, which is rebellion over who He is and His holy standard for man.

WHEN GOD CREATED ADAM AND EVE . . .

. . . they had not experienced either sin or death. God gave them the option of either obeying or disobeying Him.

God not only gave them the option to see if they would obey, but He also told them the consequences if they chose to disobey.

Genesis 2:16-17

16) "And the Lord God commanded the man, saying, 'From any tree of the garden you may eat freely;

17) "'but from the tree of the knowledge of good and evil you shall not eat, for in the day that you eat from it you shall surely die.'"

B. Adam and Eve Refused to Obey God

Freely, of their own wills, they ate of the forbidden fruit, knowing the devastating consequences of that act. God, therefore, had no choice but to put forth His judgment.

Genesis 3:19
"By the sweat of your face you shall eat bread, till you return to the ground, because from it you were taken; for you are dust, and to dust you shall return."

Man has been paying the price for sin since the fall of Adam. All of us have inherited, from our first parents, an inner nature that continues to sin.

Though Adam and Eve lived thousands of years ago, God's judgment for sin remains.

Ezekiel 18:4
"...the soul who sins will die."

C. Since all of Mankind Continues to Sin...

. . . all of mankind continues to die. Man may live his life as though he will never die, but death will follow after him until, finally, he dies and faces a holy God. God only allows men so much time to do what he pleases -- but that time runs out too quickly. When we watch ourselves and people around us getting older and getting closer to the time of death, it should continually remind us of how much God hates sin.

Romans 6:23
"For the wages of sin is death, but the free gift of God is eternal life in Christ Jesus our Lord."

III. What God Has Done About Death

It is important to realize that death goes against the very nature of God. The Bible states:

John 1:4
"In Him (Christ) was life; and the life was the light of men."

Death also goes against God's plan for our lives. God has always been concerned that we experience life to its fullest. Jesus said:

John 10:10
"...I came that they might have life, and might have it more abundantly."

Because death goes against the nature of God and His plan for our lives, let's take a look at what God has done to set us free from death and its consequences.

AS MENTIONED EARLIER, DEATH IS THE AWFUL CONSEQUENCE MAN MUST PAY FOR HIS SIN AGAINST GOD.

Since God hates sin and death, He came to earth, through Jesus Christ, to crush sin and its consequence -- death.

Jesus Christ was different from any man who ever lived. The Bible says that because Jesus was God, He was both sinless and immortal. He never committed sin and was above the curse of death.

When Jesus Christ chose to die on the cross, He voluntarily allowed God's judgment for all of mans sin to be completely placed on Him. Christ took all the judgment that we deserve for rebelling against a holy God, and paid God's total price for sin -- which is death. The Bible explains this tremendous act of love:

1 Peter 2:24
"And He Himself bore our sins in His body on the cross, that we might die to sin and live to righteousness; for by His wounds you were healed."

This amazing person, Jesus Christ (who was sinless), absorbed all of the sin that causes man to die. Because He has paid the death penalty, those who put their trust in Christ will never die!

John 5:24
"Truly, truly, I say to you, he who hears My word, and believes Him who sent Me, has eternal life, and does not come into judgment, but has passed out of death into life."

A. Christ's Death Was But for a Very Short Time

Three days after He was buried, Jesus Christ rose from the grave and conquered death for all time. He came out of the tomb with a new body that was different from the dying body we now have.

Because Christ loves us so much, He has made it possible for those who believe in Him to inherit a new body like His. The Bible calls this new body the resurrection body.

This great mystery about believers receiving new resurrection bodies is talked about in the Bible.

Philippians 3:21
"When He comes back He will take these dying bodies of ours and change them into glorious bodies like His own, using the same mighty power that He will use to conquer all else everywhere."

* *According to this verse, when will Jesus transform our dying bodies into bodies like His?*

____

* *What will enable Jesus to do this?*

____

It is, indeed, a miraculous act of love that Jesus Christ made it possible for us not to have to suffer the consequences of sin, and allow us to have a new body like His.

The Bible explains that Jesus Christ has crushed death once and for all.

1 Corinthians 15:53-54 (Living Bible)
53) "For our earthly bodies, the ones we have now that can die, must be transformed into heavenly bodies that cannot perish but will live forever.
54) "When this happens, then at last this Scripture will come true -- 'Death is swallowed up in victory.'"

B. JESUS CHRIST HAS EXPOSED SATAN'S LIE ABOUT DEATH AND DESTROYED ALL REASONS FOR US TO FEAR DEATH

Hebrews 2:14-15 (Living Bible)

14) "Since we, God's children, are human beings -- made of flesh and blood -- He became flesh and blood too by being born in human form; for only as a human being could He die and in dying break the power of the devil who had the power of death.

15) "Only in that way could He deliver those who through fear of death have been living all their lives as slaves to constant dread."

Satan is the great deceiver. It is his goal to hold men in the fear of death. Satan hates man. He knows that he is doomed to eternal judgment and wants to make as many people with him as possible. He knows that if he could get man to sin, he would have man under the fear and curse of death. He wants all men to think that death is awful and futile; therefore, convincing man that he should live only for the present. He wants man to think, "eat, drink, and be merry, for tomorrow we die".

Jesus Christ rendered Satan powerless by conquering sin and rising from the dead. He showed that eternity with God in heaven is real and can be obtained. Christians need not fear death -- because death for the believer in Christ has been defeated forever!

IV. Where Does One Go When He Dies?

LET'S ASSUME FOR A MOMENT . . .

. . . that a Christian friend of yours dies in an automobile accident. As you stand before the casket, an ever pressing question keeps coming into your mind. The questions is a basic one. "I wonder where my friend is now. Is he asleep? Is he in heaven?"

To begin with, the Bible teaches that when a Christian dies, he doesn't go to sleep, but immediately (his soul and spirit) goes to be with Christ.

Paul write to us:

2 Corinthians 5:8
"We are of good courage, I say, and prefer rather to be absent from the body and to be at home with the Lord."

A. A CHRISTIAN DIES AND IS INSTANTLY WITH JESUS

2 Corinthians 5:8 teaches us that a person who knows Jesus Christ is instantly with the Lord at the time of death.

Scripture also says that when a man dies, he sleeps. But, in every verse in which sleep is mentioned, it refers to the person's body -- not his soul.

Jesus taught that a Christian goes from one existence at death (earth) into another existence (heaven). Yet, this person who dies never loses consciousness, but finds himself in a new and wonder surrounding.

For example, because of jet travel, a person can get on a jet in Los Angeles -- where all may be warm and sunny -- and then in a few hours land in Minneapolis -- where it may be cold and snowing. In somewhat the same way, a Christian may die and instantly leave one surrounding (his body and earth) and find himself in a whole new surrounding (in the presence of the Lord)!

Jesus said to Martha:

John 11:25-26
25) "Jesus said to her, 'I am the resurrection and the life, he who believes in Me shall live even if he dies,
26) "'and everyone who lives and believes in Me shall never die. Do you believe this?'"
When Christ mentions dying here, He is refering to physical death. A person's soul may leave his body (physical death) but his soul lives on forever with Christ.

* *According to Christ's statement above, how can a person die and still live?*

____

____

IT'S FANTASTIC TO KNOW. . .

. . . that when a person asks Christ into his life, he starts a personal relationship that even death cannot stop.

It is for this reason that a Christian can look right into the face of death and stand triumphant and confident. He knows that Christ has already conquered death -- and the future is one of great joy and adventure with Christ forever!

That is why you, as a Christian, can say:

1 Corinthians 15:55
"O death, where is your victory? Death where is your sting?"

B. When Christ Returns, Old Bodies Are Made New

ANOTHER QUESTION THAT ONE MIGHT ASK . . .

. . . about the body of one who has gone to be with Christ is: "Is God finished with this person's physical body, or will God somehow use that body again in eternity?"

The Scripture explains that the believer's body goes to the grave to await the return of Jesus Christ. Christ is, of course, coming again to take the Christians off the earth. When He does come -- which could be at any moment -- He will then cause, in a miraculous way, all the bodies of the Christians who have died in the past to rise up to meet the saints in the skies.

Paul explains this overwhelming thought to us.

1 Thessalonians 4:13-18

13) "But we do not want you to be uninformed, brethren, about those who are asleep, that you may not grieve, as do the rest who have no hope.

14) "For if we believe that Jesus died and rose again, even so God will bring with Him those who have fallen asleep.

15) "For this we say to you by the word of the Lord, that we who are alive, and remain until the coming of the Lord, shall not precede those who have fallen asleep.

16) "For the Lord Himself will descend from heaven with a shout, with the voice of the archangel, and with the trumpet of God; and the dead in Christ shall rise first.

17) "Then we who are alive and remain shall be caught up together with them in the clouds to meet the Lord in the air, and thus we shall always be with the Lord.

18) "Therefore comfort one another with these words."

C. SINCE GOD THINKS OUR BODIES ARE SO IMPORTANT . . .

. . . He plans to take the bodies we now have and make them into eternal bodies when Christ comes again. While this will be a tremendous miracle, it will not be too great for God and His plans for us in heaven.

Paul speaks of this mysterious work of God, through the Holy Spirit, when he said:

1 Corinthians 15:51-53

51) "Behold, I tell you a mystery; we shall not all sleep, but we shall all be changed.

52) "in a moment, in the twinkling of an eye, at the last trumpet; for the trumpet will sound, and the dead will be raised imperishable, and we shall be changed.

53) "For this perishable must put on the imperishable, and this mortal must put on immortality."

God will take the Christian's old body and make it into one eternal, glorified, heavenly body.

When a person who knows Christ begins to understand the great plans God has for us for all eternity, he can begin to see why Paul informed us:

1 Thessalonians 4:14
"For if we believe that Jesus died and rose again, even so God will bring with Him those who have fallen asleep in Jesus."

There is no doubt that death causes heartbreak. Because death is the penalty for sin, it will always cause pain as long as we live on this earth. It is not wrong to cry at a funeral because our tears are often lonely tears of missing the one who has left us. Jesus Christ wept at a funeral for He hates death more than anyone else. But, because of the great work of Jesus Christ at the cross and resurrection, death has been conquered. What awaits the Christian in death is something so wonderful, so meaningful, that all true believers should, by faith, be able to say along with the Apostle Paul:

2 Corinthians 5:8
"We are of good courage, I say, and prefer rather to be absent from the body, and to be at home with the Lord."

NOTES

TODAY MORE THAN EVER BEFORE STUDENTS ARE ASKING THE QUESTIONS, -- "IS CHRISTIANITY PRACTICAL?" "WHAT WILL IT DO FOR ME?"

THE FOLLOWING SERIES OF MANUALS DEAL WITH GOD'S ANSWERS TO STUDENTS' NEEDS IN A PRACTICAL WAY.

CHAPTER TITLE	DESCRIPTION
The Importance of Your New Life	*This chapter deals with our newly established relationship with God through Jesus.*
The Importance of God's Love and Forgiveness	*Learning to deal with sin on a daily basis and understanding the completeness of God's forgiveness is discussed in this section.*
The Importance of Your Trials	*Understanding trials, why we have them, and how God uses them are the topics in this chapter.*
The Importance of The Word	*This important section reaffirms the importance and reliability of God's Word in the believers life.*
The Importance of Your Quiet Time	*Spending time daily in God's Word is essential to spiritual growth. Practical "how to's" are given in this chapter.*
The Importance of Your Prayer	*A scriptural and motivational basis for prayer is discussed in this chapter.*
The Importance of the Spirit-Filled Life	*The key to this section is its simplicity in answering the questions--Who is the Holy Spirit? Why did He come? What is His role?*
The Importance of Walking in the Spirit	*How to allow God Himself to live His life through us on a daily basis is discussed in this section.*
The Importance of Your Fellowship	*This chapter explains the importance of the Christian student spending time with other Christians.*
The Importance of Sharing Your Faith	*The goal of this chapter is to introduce students to the joy and excitement of introducing others to Jesus Christ and motivate them in a positive way to witness.*

CHAPTER TITLE	DESCRIPTION
The Importance of Obedience	*This chapter deals with our responsibility to God in regard to our living a successful Christian life.*
Learning to Obey God	*This continues the theme of chapter 1, with specific application concerning our being obedient.*
Worship	*The importance of worship as a lifestyle is discussed here.*
The Christian and the Lordship of Christ	*This chapter is the very essence of the Christian life. Learning to let Christ be Lord is the key to a successful lifestyle.*
The Christian Life and Endurance	*Many Christians start out in a blaze of glory but end in disaster. This chapter deals with the Christian and endurance.*
The Responsibility of Love	*Learning to love one another in Christ is dealt with in this chapter.*
Our Responsibility Toward Other Christians	*The importance of our relationships with other Christians is discussed here.*
How to Start Your Own Ministry	*Jesus taught us not to only hear His words. This chapter gives helpful and creative ways of starting your own ministry.*

CHAPTER TITLE	DESCRIPTION
The Importance of Understanding The Bible, A Counselling Book	*The value and wisdom the Bible can shed on everyday life is discussed here.*
The Importance of Knowing God's Will	*Whom should I marry? What school should I attend? What vocation should I pursue? are questions this chapter will help answer.*
The Importance of a Balanced Self-Image	*This chapter shares how God sees us and how to form a proper self-image.*
The Importance of Dealing with Loneliness	*One of the biggest problems the American st faces is loneliness. This chapter gives answers on how to deal with this problem.*
The Importance of Understanding Parents	*Few relationships affect our lives as do our relationship with our parents. The problems and solutions are shared in this chapter.*
The Importance of Understanding Sex	*This section deals with the rationale of why God's saying what He does about sex.*
The Importance of Understanding Dating	*This chapter gives insight into questions such as--What are the problems in dating? What should I look for in a date? Does God have a plan for my date life?*
The Importance of Understanding Love	*This work deals with some of the difference between love and infatuation.*
The Importance of Clearing The Mind	*The importance of thinking pure and Godly thoughts are discussed in this chapter.*
The Importance of Dealing With Temptation	*Being tempted and knowing who tempts us is not always easy to recognize. This chapter gives practical insights in the whole area of temptation.*

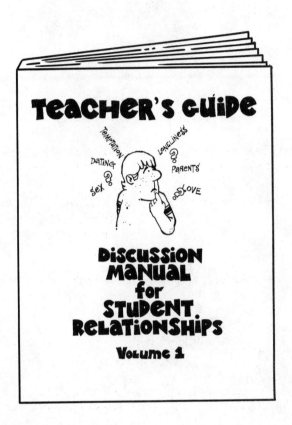

Overhead Transparencies

for Volume I of the *Discussion Manual for Student Relationships*

You get . . .

- 78 Large Cartoon Pictures Right Out of the Manual
- Helpful Teaching Headlines
- Plenty of Space for Your Notes
- Colorful
- Reasonably Priced

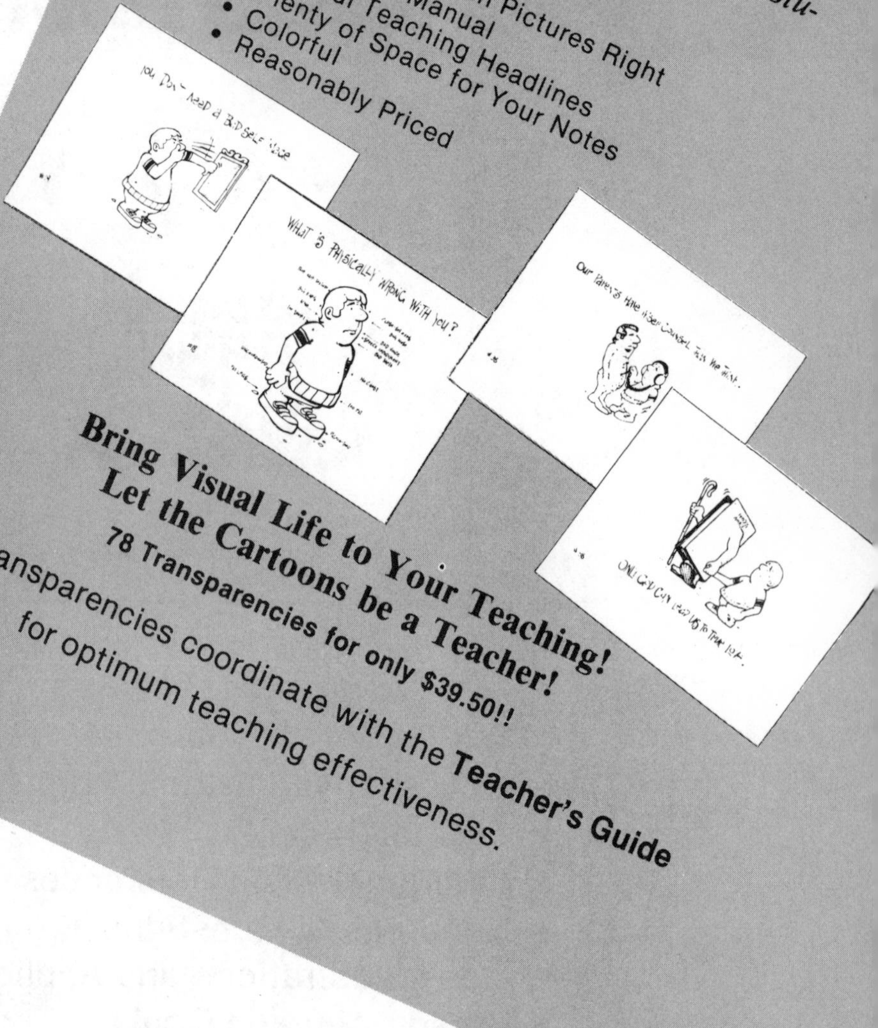

Bring Visual Life to Your Teaching!
Let the Cartoons be a Teacher!

78 Transparencies for only $39.50!!

All 78 transparencies coordinate with the **Teacher's Guide** for optimum teaching effectiveness.

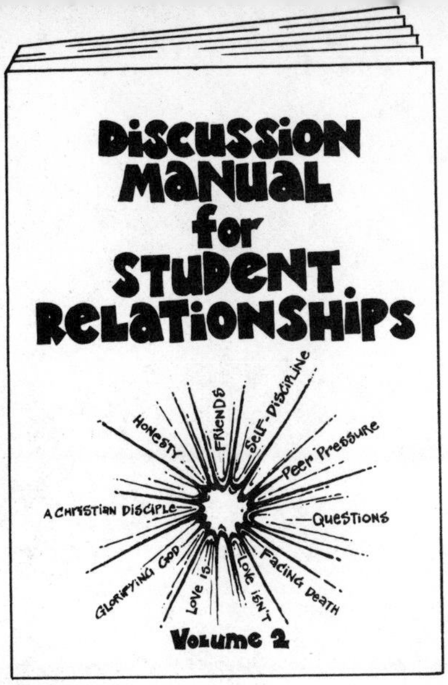

Chapter Title	Description
How to Glorify God	Glorifying God and how to do it can be difficult to understand and teach. This simple chapter gets to the heart of glorifying God.
Discipleship	This chapter shares the answers to the questions, What does it mean to be a disciple of Jesus? Where do I begin?
Love	Using I Corinthians 13 as its guide this chapter clearly defines what true love is.
What Love Is Not	Again using the love chapter as its basis this chapter explains what love is not.
Questions on Dating	The author of the manual Dawson McAllister, answers questions high school students across the country are asking on dating.
Peer Group Pressure	One of the strongest influences in our lives is the thoughts and actions of our peers towards us. In this discussion we learn how to deal with this pressure.
Making Friends	This chapter stresses the importance of learning how to make friends and the type of friends God desires for us to have.
Honesty	Honesty is often rejected in a world where personal gain is more important than trustworthiness. Here we investigate the results of being dishonest and the benefits of honesty.

This book is a must for the youth library.